LET'S LANGUAGE DEVELOPMENT TEACHER'S MANUAL

National Textbook Company
NTC a division of *NTC Publishing Group* • Lincolnwood, Illinois USA

1994 Printing

Published by National Textbook Company, a division of NTC Publishing Group.

Manufactured in the United States of America.

3 4 5 6 7 8 9 0 VP 9 8 7 6 5 4 3 2

Contents

Preface

This teacher's manual was designed for use with the *Let's Learn* Picture Dictionaries, the *Let's Learn* Language Development Transparencies, or with both. The picture dictionaries and transparencies can be employed independently to help students develop their vocabulary and communication skills. Used in conjunction, they provide an even more versatile and useful classroom tool.

The transparencies contain the same scenes and pictures as the picture dictionaries. If you use the two together, you may use the transparencies for initial presentation and the book to introduce reading and writing with the target vocabulary. Or you may prefer to use the books and transparencies for presentation of vocabulary and then use the transparencies to evaluate students' mastery of the words.

This manual contains one unit for each scene in the picture dictionaries and transparencies. Note that the scenes can be presented to your class in any order. Because they are not arranged in order of difficulty, you can introduce them when and as they fit the sequence of your language program.

The activities in this manual were created to help you make the most of the *Let's Learn* Picture Dictionaries and Language Development Transparencies. They will help you introduce, as well as reinforce, the vocabulary illustrated in the thirty-two scenes of the books and transparencies and provide students with many opportunities to practice using the words both orally and in writing. Many of the activities provide contexts in which students can use the words naturally in communicative situations. In addition, for each scene there are simple, controlled activities that help prepare students for the more open-ended tasks. The wide variety of activities allows you to choose those that match your students' proficiency level.

The activities in this manual are appropriate for teaching all the languages in which the *Let's Learn* Picture Dictionaries are available or for any language. Although the directions and examples are given in English, they are designed to be adaptable to any target language.

Introduction

This introduction explains how the suggested activities for the various units in this manual can be implemented in the classroom. In addition, it presents some standard activities that are appropriate for use with all or most of the units.

The introduction has three sections:

1. Initial Presentation of Words

This section contains suggestions for introducing the pictures and vocabulary words in the scenes to the students.

2. Parts of the Unit

This section describes the structure of the teacher's manual units. It explains the pedagogy behind the parts of the units and contains concrete suggestions for their implementation in the classroom.

3. Reinforcement/Evaluation

This section contains suggestions for evaluation of student mastery of the vocabulary once students have been presented the words and have done some of the class activities.

INITIAL PRESENTATION OF WORDS

1. Introduce the Situation in the Picture

To help students understand the context for the words and to stimulate their interest in the activities, introduce them to the situation in the picture. To do this, have students identify the place or situation depicted in the scene, tell about whether they have ever been to the place pictured, and point out things in the scene that they know, that they don't know or understand, or that interest them.

2. Presenting the Words

The pictures, both of the situation and of the individual objects, provide an effective context for initially presenting the words and helping students understand their meaning.

You might want to present five to ten words at a time, or if students are familiar with many of the words, you might be able to present all or most of the words in a unit in one session. Here are some techniques for the initial presentation of words that are appropriate for all the units:

a. Have students look at the large picture and identify all the objects that they know in the picture. For the words with which students are unfamiliar, point to the object, say the name, and have students repeat it. Then have students look at the small pictures and identify the objects that they know or that they have just learned. Note that the transparencies do not have the names of the objects printed next to the small pictures. If you are using the transparencies, you may eventually wish to provide students with a list of vocabulary found in a scene (each unit in the teacher's manual begins with a word list). If you are using the transparencies and picture dictionary in conjunction, you can have students look at the small pictures in the book and read the words you have just presented.

b. Next name an object and have students point to it in either the large or small picture, saying the name. Then point to an object and have students name the object you are pointing to.

Note: It is a good idea to introduce the appropriate article (e.g., a/an) with nouns, since it may vary with the gender of the noun.

Further Presentation Activities

Location: Once students have been introduced to the names of several objects and if students know some of the basic prepositions in the target language, the large picture can be used as a prompt for naming objects. This activity will be useful in reviewing words and will be appropriate for most units.

Examples:

Who is in front of the desk? *(teacher)*

What's next to the desk? *(wastebasket)*

Words in Context: For each word (or just key words or difficult words), present a sentence or two that illustrates its meaning. Such sentences can reinforce and clarify the meaning of the word and help students learn how it is used syntactically. Students can repeat the sentence. In addition, in many cases, they can "act out" the sentence to give a "physical" reinforcement to students' visual and oral recognition of the word.

Examples:

You use *scissors* to cut paper. One piece. Cut, cut. Two pieces. *(Students can imitate the action of cutting to reinforce their understanding and retention of the word "scissors.")*

A *mail carrier* brings the mail to your house. The mail carrier puts letters in your mailbox. *(Students can imitate the action of putting letters into a mailbox.)*

You use a *steering wheel* to drive. *(Students imitate driving a car with the steering wheel.)*

You should prepare sentences like these in advance. Such sentences will be particularly useful for objects with which students may not be very familiar.

In addition, the Words in Context sentences can be "chanted." Chanting is a technique in which students say sentences rhythmically to practice the intonation pattern of the target language and internalize vocabulary and sentence structures. Techniques for presenting chants are described under Group Activities on page xi.

Pantomimes: Pantomimes can also be useful in serving as prompts for review of words and in adding a "physical" dimension to the visual/oral learning of words. For example, you can act out using some of the objects introduced in the picture.

Examples: putting clothes on a hanger and hanging them up to elicit the word *hanger,* sawing to elicit the word *saw,* and so on.

Once students are familiar with the words in the unit, they can do the pantomimes. In addition, the pantomimes can eventually be extended so that students say complete sentences to describe what is being pantomimed, using the words in context and associating them with appropriate verbs and nouns.

Examples:

She's putting detergent into the washing machine.

She's a pharmacist. She's putting pills into a bottle.

Word Cards: To help students study words, have them prepare index cards with the unit words. Students should write a word on each card and illustrate it, if possible. These cards can be used to help students review words, as well as any sentences they have learned that illustrate the meaning of the words. Example: Saw—We use a saw to cut wood. These cards can also be used in some of the group activities suggested in the various units in this manual. For example, they can be used in the Classifying section in the Group Activities, with students grouping the cards that fit into each of the suggested categories.

Units in the Teacher's Manual: In addition to the activities just suggested, two parts in this teacher's manual for each of the units can also be effective in the initial presentation. These sections are Questions about the Picture and Action Stories. The nature of each of these parts is explained in the next section, Parts of the Unit.

PARTS OF THE UNIT

Each unit in this teacher's manual has six parts:

Questions about the Picture

Action Stories

Group Activities

Writing

Focus on Language

Vocabulary

What each of these parts contains and how each can be implemented in the classroom is explained below.

The Questions about the Picture, Group Activities, and Writing sections all take the following approach: the first activities are relatively simple and all students who have learned the words should be able to complete them, no matter what their proficiency in the target language. Later activities usually require that students have basic speaking/writing skills. The Action Stories are appropriate for all levels of language proficiency, and most Focus on Language activities can be used from the high beginner level up.

Questions about the Picture

This section can be used as part of the initial presentation of words or once the initial presentation is completed. The section is *not* intended to give an exhaustive list of questions but rather to illustrate the types of questions that can be used in connection with the unit vocabulary.

The section proceeds from relatively simple questions that involve simple identification to open-ended questions designed to elicit student discussion. In addition, there typically are questions that ask students to interpret various situations in the picture.

Suggestions for initial presentation questions: For initial presentation, you can ask simple questions incorporating definitions of objects or people: On what do you sleep? *(bed)* Who flies an airplane? *(pilot)* Then proceed to the questions that require grouping objects: Name two buildings on a farm. Name six animals on a farm. Then proceed to uses of objects: What do you use toothpaste for? *(I use it to clean my teeth.)*

In addition, for very beginning students, the questions might be presented in students' native language, rather than in the target language.

Action Stories

Action Stories incorporate the principles of Total Physical Response, in which students' learning of language is enhanced by their performing actions. In the Action Stories, students are given a series of related commands to follow. The commands involve the students in acting out the meanings of words they are learning. This gives a kinesthetic dimension to vocabulary/language learning, which can be particularly effective with younger students. In addition, students are learning the appropriate verbs and syntax to talk about the objects whose names they are learning.

The units in this manual contain possible topics for Action Stories. A sample Action Story for one of the topics is also presented for each unit. The Action Story contains, and illustrates the meaning of, many of the vocabulary words in the unit. You can adapt the story for use in the target language or produce a story based on one of the other possible topics listed. The stories you present should contain related groups of words from the unit. In many cases, the words that could be incorporated into the Action Story are given in parentheses after the possible story topic.

In presenting the Action Stories, you can follow this technique:

1. Say the statements and act out the story yourself.
2. Next have students act out the story with you, imitating your actions as you give the commands.
3. Then have students follow the commands with no visual prompts.
4. You might then want to write the commands on the board and have students repeat/read them.
5. Next have individual students give the commands to the class.
6. Finally have students work in pairs and orally give the commands to each other.

Wherever possible, have students use actual objects rather than just pantomiming.

Group Activities

Group activities are intended to reinforce vocabulary and lead students to use the words in meaningful contexts. The group activities range from relatively simple activities that require one-word responses to open-ended activities such as interviews and role plays. The number of activities you present from this part depends on the level of proficiency of your class. Many of the activities can be adapted for presentation *either* to the whole class or to small groups.

Here are suggestions for presenting some of the group activities commonly found in the units:

Classifying. Almost all of the group activities begin with a classifying activity that requires students to group words from the lesson. This is intended as a pair or small-group activity. Often the way words are classified can differ and the differences can be justified. Encourage such discussion if students are sufficiently proficient in the language.

If students have prepared word cards for the lessons, the cards can be used to facilitate this activity. Students can group the cards for each classification. Otherwise, students can write down the words for each category under the appropriate heading.

Chanting. Chanting is a technique in which students say sentences rhythmically. The goal of chanting is to have students practice the intonation pattern of the target language and internalize vocabulary and sentence structures. You produce simple chants by having students repeat key words or phrases in rhythmic patterns.

Example:

In the dining room, room, room, all the family eats, eats, eats.

In the summer, summer, summer, butterflies fly, fly, fly.

In the units, many of the chants suggested call for sentences that give definitions of the words. You can prepare the sentences to chant as a group activity, producing a class definition/sentence. Then, say the sentence orally. You can modify it if necessary so that it is suitable to chant, that is, so that words that be repeated at appropriate pauses. Have students repeat the sentences as you or they produce them. Once all the sentences are produced, review them by having students chant the appropriate sentence for the word you point to.

Role Play/Interviews. The suggested role plays and interviews in this teacher's manual are best suited to students who have some proficiency in the language. However, you can simplify the tasks so that they can be successfully used even by high beginning students. Here are two suggestions: (1) Present students with a few model questions and answers, which they can use in their own role plays. (2) Take one (or both) of the roles and present the role play/interview to the class to provide a sample of what to say.

Information-Gap Activities. Several lessons have information-gap activities, in which the words from the unit form the basis of the information to be found. Information-gap activities are designed to be completed by pairs of students. For these activities, two different columns of words and phrases are presented. You use these columns to prepare two different sheets, each containing information missing from the other. You might put the first column on one sheet, and the second on the other. To vary the activity, particularly for students who are more proficient, have each sheet contain some of the material from each column.

Pass out a different sheet to each student in the pair. The students' task is to complete their sheets by getting the information on their partner's sheets. They do this by asking each other questions, without showing their sheets to each other. In most of the information-gap activities, sample language for students to use to elicit information is provided.

Writing

Writing activities help students to reinforce their knowledge of words and to use the words in context. The activities range from making simple lists to using the words in creative stories. Many of the activities can be used as whole-group, small-group, or independent activities.

Even if students' level of proficiency in the target language is not high, most of the writing activities can still be used. They can be presented as whole-class activities, in which students orally make suggestions for a story that you write down on the board. The result is a story produced by the class. For more proficient classes, the class story can become a model for students to use to write their own stories.

Almost all the units begin with one or two activities in which students just have to list words. These can be completed even by very beginning students. The suggested drawing activities are most appropriate for primary classes.

Focus on Language

This section gives suggestions for presenting a language point that relates to the words or situations in the unit. In some cases, phrases or structures that are related to the pictured situation are presented. For example, for the unit "In a Restaurant," polite requests are suggested for review. In some cases, grammar points are suggested for presentation or review.

Vocabulary

This section contains lists of the vocabulary in the unit (the words for each of the small pictures) in English, Spanish, French, German, and Italian. You may use these lists for your own reference or, if you are using only the transparencies to present vocabulary, these lists can help you make up vocabulary lists for your students.

REINFORCEMENT/EVALUATION

A wide variety of activities can be used to review the vocabulary or to evaluate students' mastery of it. These should be presented once students have been introduced to the words and have practiced them orally and in writing.

Here are some basic activities to review the words and evaluate students' retention of them:

1. Stimulus/Word Response

Write a list of words from the unit on the board. Have students number their papers. Show the unit transparency and point to an object in the transparency. If you are using the picture dictionary, pantomime a word. Students are to write the word illustrated on their papers. To make the task more difficult, do not provide students with the word list.

2. Classifying/Listing

Have students do classifying/listing activities similar to the ones in the units.

Examples:

List all the things you can write with.

List all the things that have to do with a clock.

3. Sentence Completion

Provide ten to fifteen sentences for the students to complete for each unit.

Examples:

A person who does your nails is a __manicurist__.

You use __shampoo__ to wash your hair.

My friend's hair is not curly; it is __straight__.

4. What Doesn't Belong

Prepare five to ten lists of four or five items each. Students are to circle the item that doesn't belong.

Examples:

1. bangs, mustache, ponytail, crew cut	Answer:	mustache
2. shampoo, mousse, hair spray, wavy	Answer:	wavy
3. freckles, mascara, lipstick, powder	Answer:	freckles
4. black, blond, braid, brown	Answer:	braid
5. wavy, straight, curly, curlers	Answer:	curlers

5. Memory Game

Once students are familiar with the picture and words, have students list as many items as they can remember from the picture.

6. Picture Description

Have students describe the picture. Encourage them to include as many of the words they have learned from the unit as they can. Also encourage them to write connected sentences.

Example: The picture shows a doctor's office. A boy is sitting on the examining table. He has an arm in a sling. The doctor is examining the patient, etc.

1. Our Classroom

QUESTIONS ABOUT THE PICTURE

1. Name two things you need to draw a picture.
2. Name two things you use to work at the chalkboard.
3. *(lower right)* Name all the things on the first desk.
4. *(upper right)* What is the girl at the chalkboard doing?
5. *(center)* What is in front of the window?
6. *(center)* What are the children in the second row doing?
7. *(left)* Name the things on the teacher's desk.
8. Tell about the wastebasket.
9. Is the classroom in the picture like your classroom? How is it the same? How is it different?
10. Are the things the children are doing the same as things you do in school? What things are the same? What things are different?

ACTION STORIES

Possible topics: painting/drawing a picture, watering the cactus (not too much water), using a calculator, making decorations *(scissors, crayons, paint, paintbrush)*

Example: Painting a picture

1. You are going to paint a picture. 2. Get a paintbrush and paints. 3. Put a piece of paper on an easel. 4. Pick up your paintbrush. 5. Dip your brush into the paint. 6. Paint something on the paper. 7. Take your picture off the easel. 8. Get a piece of cellophane tape. 9. Put it on top of the picture. 10. Tape the picture on the bulletin board.

GROUP ACTIVITIES

1. Classifying

Have students name as many objects from the picture as they can for each of the following categories: things to write with, things on the wall, things you put in your desk, things you use to draw, things you use when you write on the chalkboard, things you use to put other things together, living things, things that make noise, things that have something to do with math.

2. Guessing Game

You or a student describes the location of an object in the picture, and other students name the object being described. Have students use the prepositions *next to, in front of, in back of.*

Example: It's in front of the window. *(the aquarium)* It's next to the desk and in front of the easel. *(wastebasket)*

3. Word Association

Have students list all the words that they can associate with each of the following words: *cut, paper, addition, clock, erase, world, write, color, circle, water.* Have students explain the reasons they have for associating items.

4. Word Hunt

Divide the class into groups of four. Have each group choose a name. Have them write as many words as they remember from the picture on separate pieces of paper, together with the group's name. Once this task is finished, have students place words on or next to the actual object in the classroom. Once this is done, examine the location of the papers and determine which group has remembered and located the most items.

5. Role Play

Present the following role plays to students:

a. There is a new student in your class. There's something very unusual about the student. He/she comes from another planet! As a result, the student doesn't know how to use the everyday things in the classroom. Help the new student use the things needed to get through a class lesson. Explain the use of pencil, paper, crayon, etc.
b. You are the girl in the second row. Tell what you are doing.

6. Debate

Have students discuss what animal they would like as a class pet. Encourage discussion of issues such as caring for the pet on vacation, how interesting the animal is to watch, etc. At the end of the discussion, take a vote on the most popular pet.

WRITING

Have students do these activities independently or as whole-class or group activities.

1. List the things that you have with you in your classroom.
2. Prepare an alphabet book. *(Instruct students to write each letter on a separate page. Then, depending on their level of proficiency, have them draw or find pictures of one or more objects that begin with each letter.)*
3. Write about what you do in a typical day at school.
4. Write about how your classroom is different from the classroom in the picture.
5. Write about an unusual day in your classroom. It may be a day on which someone visits your class. Or you can make up a story about an unusual day: for example, the day the frog got loose in your room.

FOCUS ON LANGUAGE

Have students review the letters of the alphabet in the target language. You may want to have students write and repeat the letters. If you have recordings available or know any alphabet songs, present them to the class.

VOCABULARY

Our Classroom	En classe	Nuestra aula	Unser Klassenzimmer	Nostra Classe
teacher (m.)	l'instituteur	el maestro	der Lehrer	il maestro
teacher (f.)	l'institutrice	la maestra	die Lehrerin	la maestra
student (m.)	l'élève	el alumno	der Schüler	l'alunno
student (f.)	l'élève	la alumna	die Schülerin	l'alunna
map	la carte	el mapa	die Landkarte	la carta geografica
chalkboard	le tableau noir	la pizarra	die Wandtafel	la lavagna
chalk	la craie	la tiza	die Kreide	il gesso
(chalkboard) eraser	l'éponge à effacer	el borrador	der Schwamm	il cancellino
trash	les déchets	la basura	der Abfall	la spazzatura
wastebasket	la corbeille à papier	la papelera	der Papierkorb	il cestino
stapler	l'agrafeuse	la grapadora	die Heftmaschine	l'aggraffatrice
staples	les agrafes	las grapas	die Heftklammern	le graffette
teacher's desk	le bureau du maître	el escritorio	das Lehrerpult	la cattedra
calendar	le calendrier	el calendario	der Kalender	il calendario
cellophane tape	le ruban adhésif	la cinta adhesiva	der Tesafilm	il cellofan
notebook	le cahier	el cuaderno	das Heft	il quaderno
bookcase	l'étagère	la estantería	das Bücherregal	lo scaffale
bulletin board	le tableau d'affichage	el tablón de noticias	die Anzeigetafel	la bacheca
arithmetic problem	le problème d'arithmétique	el problema aritmético	die Rechenaufgabe	il problema d'aritmetica
calculator	la calculatrice	la calculadora	der Rechner	il calcolatore
alphabet	l'alphabet	el alfabeto	das Alphabet	l'alfabeto
easel	le chevalet	el caballete de pintor	die Staffelei	il cavalletto
protractor	le rapporteur	el prolongador	der Winkelmesser	il goniometro
pen	le stylo	el bolígrafo	der Kugelschreiber	la penna
colored pencils	les crayons de couleur	los lápices de color	die Farbstifte	le matite colorate
pupil desk	le pupitre	el pupitre	das Pult	il banco
aquarium	l'aquarium	el acuario	das Aquarium	l'acquario
fish	le poisson	el pez	der Fisch	il pesce
loudspeaker	le haut-parleur	el altavoz	der Lautsprecher	l'altoparlante
book	le livre	el libro	das Buch	il libro

rug	le tapis	la alfombra	der Teppich	il tappeto
ruler	la règle	la regla	das Lineal	la regola
scissors	les ciseaux	las tijeras	die Schere	le forbici
bell	la cloche	la campana	die Glocke	la campanella
hole punch	la perforeuse	la taladradora de papel	der Locher	la perforatrice per carta
compass	le compas	el compás	der Zirkel	il compasso
(pencil) eraser	la gomme	la goma de borrar	der Radiergummi	la gomma
pencil	le crayon	el lápiz	der Bleistift	la matita
pencil sharpener	le taille-crayon	el sacapuntas	der Spitzer	il temperamatite
clock	l'horloge	el reloj	die Uhr	l'orologio
hand (of clock)	l'aiguille	la manecilla	der Zeiger	la lancetta
numbers	les nombres	los números	die Nummern	i numeri
cactus	le cactus	el cacto	der Kaktus	il cactus
plant	la plante	la planta	die Pflanze	la pianta
glue	la colle	la cola	der Klebstoff	la colla
globe	le globe terrestre	el globo terráqueo	der Globus	il globo
picture	le dessin	el cuadro	das Bild	il quadro
paint	la peinture	la pintura	die Farbe	il colore
paintbrush	le pinceau	el pincel	der Pinsel	il pennello
paper	le papier	el papel	das Papier	la carta
crayon	le crayon de couleur	el creyón	der Buntstift	il pastello

2. Our House

QUESTIONS ABOUT THE PICTURE

1. In what room do you eat/sleep/take a bath/watch TV?
2. *(top right)* Name three things in the bedroom at the top right.
3. Name three things that play music.
4. *(top center)* What is the man in the bathroom doing?
5. *(living room)* What is the person in the living room doing?
6. What do you use to wake you up?
7. What do you use to dry your face?
8. What do you use to hang your clothes?
9. How is where you and your friends live different from the house in the picture? Do most people you know live in apartments? Do the places have more than one floor?
10. What things do you have in your living room?

ACTION STORIES

Possible topics: how to put on and play a cassette tape *(cassette player, tape),* getting ready for school

Example: Getting ready for school

1. Ring! Ring! The alarm is ringing. 2. It's time to get up. 3. Push the button and turn the alarm off. 4. Push the sheet and the blanket off you. 5. Get out of bed. 6. Walk to the bathroom. 7. Wash your face. 8. Dry it with the towel. 9. Walk back to your bedroom. 10. Walk to the closet. 11. Take your clothes off the hangers. 12. Put your clothes on.

GROUP ACTIVITIES

1. Classifying

Have students name as many objects from the picture as they can for each of the following categories: things you can sit on, things on a bed, things to put in a window, things on a wall, things that make noise or music, things in the bedroom, parts of the house that are outside, furniture.

2. Memory Game

Have students work in pairs or small groups. They are not to look at the picture. Have them write down the names of (or draw) as many rooms and objects from the rooms as they can remember from the picture. Have groups compare their answers. To extend the activity, have students list other words that relate to each room (e.g., picture, cabinet, stereo, dining room table).

3. Chanting

Prepare sentences that tell the use of each room and/or the objects in the room. You may want to do this together with the students.

Examples:

Places: We eat in the dining room. We cook in the kitchen. We take a bath in the bathroom.
Uses of objects: My alarm clock wakes me up. I listen to music on my cassette player.

Using appropriate sentences, make up chants (in which key words are repeated) for students to repeat/perform. Example: I sleep, sleep, sleep in my bedroom, bedroom, bedroom.

4. Be an Interior Decorator

Have students work in pairs. Have them draw rectangles to represent various rooms in a house and label them. Have students draw various pieces of furniture, writing the names on the pieces. Have the groups explain their drawings to the class.

WRITING

Have students do these activities independently or as whole-class or group activities.

1. Draw a picture of a house, either a house you know or a house you make up. Label the rooms.
2. *(Cut pictures of rooms from magazines for this activity.)* Name the room shown in the picture and list all the things you can name in it.
3. You have just moved to the house in the picture. Write a letter about what the house is like to a friend in another town.
4. You have your own room, and you can have anything you want in it. Write about what your special room is like. (Would it have posters? a stereo? games?)

5. Think of a character you have read about. What do you think his or her room looks like?

FOCUS ON LANGUAGE

1. Review the patterns in the target language that students need to describe things and their locations.

   Examples:

   There is a bed in the bedroom.

   There are pictures on the wall.

To present the structure, point to objects in the picture and in the classroom, and then have students describe locations of objects.

2. Review the phrases in the target language for *turn on/turn off*. Have students name things that they can turn on and turn off and pantomime the actions of doing so.

VOCABULARY

Our House	Notre maison	Nuestra casa	Unser Haus	Nostra casa
floor	le plancher	el piso	der Fußboden	il pavimento
wall	le mur	la pared	die Wand	la parete
ceiling	le plafond	el techo	die Decke	il soffitto
door	la porte	la puerta	die Tür	la porta
shelf	l'étagère	el estante	das Regal	lo scaffale
closet	le placard	el ropero	der Wandschrank	l'armadio a muro
hanger	le cintre	el colgadero	der Kleiderbügel	l'attaccapanni
window	la fenêtre	la ventana	das Fenster	la finestra
stairs	l'escalier	la escalera	die Treppe	le scale
medicine cabinet	la pharmacie	el gabinete de medicina	die Hausapotheke	l'armadietto farmaceutico
bathtub	la baignoire	la tina	die Badewanne	la vasca
shower	la douche	la ducha	die Dusche	la doccia
towel	la serviette	la toalla	das Handtuch	l'asciugamano
toilet	la toilette	el inodoro	die Toilette	la toletta
toilet paper	le papier hygiénique	el papel higiénico	das Toilettenpapier	la carta igienica
bed	le lit	la cama	das Bett	il letto
blanket	la couverture	la manta	die Decke	la coperta di lana
sheet	le drap	la sábana	das Bettuch	il lenzuolo
pillow	l'oreiller	la almohada	das Kopfkissen	il guanciale
mirror	le miroir	el espejo	der Spiegel	lo specchio
vase	le vase	el florero	die Vase	il vaso
night table	la table de nuit	la mesa de noche	der Nachttisch	il tavolo
alarm clock	le réveille-matin	el despertador	der Wecker	la sveglia
rocking chair	la chaise à bascule	la mecedora	der Schaukelstuhl	la sedia a dondolo
curtains	les rideaux	las cortinas	die Vorhänge	le tendine
venetian blinds	les jalousies	las persianas	die Jalousien	le persiane
poster	l'affiche	el cartel	das Plakat	il cartellone
chimney	la cheminée	la chimenea	der Kamin	il camino
roof	le toit	el tejado	das Dach	il tetto
armchair	le fauteuil	el sillón	der Sessel	la poltrona
sofa	le canapé	el sofá	das Sofa	il divano

television	la télévision	la televisión	das Fernseher	il televisore
radio	la radio	el radio	das Radio	la radio
fireplace	la cheminée	la chimenea	der Kamin	il focolare
carpet	le tapis	la alfombra	der Teppich	il tappeto
footstool	le tabouret	el banquillo	die Fußbank	il posapiedi
telephone	le téléphone	el teléfono	das Telefon	il telefono
lamp	la lampe	la lámpara	die Lampe	la lampada
dresser	la commode	el tocador	die Frisierkommode	la toletta
record	le disque	el disco	die Schallplatte	il disco
record player	le tourne-disque	el tocadiscos	der Plattenspieler	il giradischi
compact disc	le disc compact	el disco compacto	die Compact disc	il compact disc
videocassette player	le magnétoscope	el pasador de videos	der Videorecorder	il videoregistratore
cassette tape	la cassette	el casete	die Kassette	la cassetta
cassette player	le magnétophone	la grabadora	der Kassettenrecorder	il magnetofono
bedroom	la chambre à coucher	el dormitorio	das Schlafzimmer	la camera da letto
bathroom	la salle de bain	el cuarto de baño	das Badezimmer	la stanza da bagno
living room	le salon	la sala	das Wohnzimmer	il salotto
dining room	la salle à manger	el comedor	das Eßzimmer	la sala da pranzo
kitchen	la cuisine	la cocina	die Küche	la cucina

3. The Kitchen/The Utility Room

QUESTIONS ABOUT THE PICTURES

1. Name two places you put things to keep them cold.
2. Name some things you use to cook.
3. Name four tools you can use in the house.
4. *(kitchen)* What is the woman doing?
5. *(kitchen)* What is the boy doing? Is he being careful?
6. What is the difference between a stove and a microwave oven?
7. Why do you use a vacuum cleaner, a drill, etc.?
8. What tools can you use to make something out of wood; for example, a picture frame or a birdhouse? What is the use of each tool?
9. How are houses in your neighborhood different from the house in the pictures?
10. What chores or work do you do in your house? Do you help in the kitchen or with the laundry?

ACTION STORIES

Possible topics: how to make breakfast *(toaster, dishes, pan, refrigerator),* how to do the laundry *(washing machine, laundry detergent),* to make ice cubes *(faucet, sink),* how to cook an egg *(pan, spatula),* cleaning the kitchen *(broom, dustpan, dishes, sink, dishwasher)*

Example: How to make a simple breakfast

1. It's time for breakfast. 2. Go to the refrigerator and open the door. 3. Look for the orange juice. 4. Take the bottle from the refrigerator and pour yourself a glass. 5. Go to the bread drawer and open it. 6. Get a slice of bread. 7. Close the drawer. 8. Go to the toaster. 9. Put the slice of bread into the toaster. 10. Press down the button. 11. Wait a minute. 12. Pop! The toast is ready. Let's eat!

GROUP ACTIVITIES

1. Classifying

Have students name as many objects from the picture as they can for each of the following categories: things you can use to make breakfast, things you use to do the laundry, things you can use to clean the floor, things that go into a toolbox, things you need to put a picture on a wall, things that need electricity to run, pans, things you can use to cook an egg, things you use to iron.

2. Pantomime

Pantomime actions that involve the objects in the pictures. Have students guess the objects you are working with. Examples: turning on a faucet, putting dishes in dishwasher, using a spatula, hammering a nail with a hammer, drilling a hole with a drill, sawing a board. Extend the activity by using the pantomimes to introduce the verbs that go with the objects. Then have individual students do pantomimes for the class to guess. Encourage the class to answer in complete sentences. Example: She's putting detergent into the washing machine.

3. Two-Part Chants

Prepare pairs of sentences that name the items in the picture and describe their uses. Point to each item in the picture, and have students repeat the sentences. Eventually just point to the item. One half of the class identifies the item, and the other half supplies the definition.

Examples:

This is a faucet.	Water comes out of the faucet.
This is a microwave oven.	It cooks food quickly.
This is a broom.	You use it to clean the floor.
This is a saw.	You use it to cut a board.

4. Group Story

With the students, decide on a meal to make. Then, together, write a "process" story listing the steps to make the meal.

5. Discussion

Have you ever helped to cook or do the laundry or made something with tools? Lead students in a discussion of these topics.

WRITING

Have students do these activities independently or as whole-class or group activities.

1. List things you can use to make breakfast.
2. You can design a new kitchen. Draw what the kitchen will look like. Label the objects in your picture.
3. Write about a time you cooked or used everyday tools to make something. Prompts: What did you make? Did you have any problems?

FOCUS ON LANGUAGE

Review the verb/noun combinations needed to talk about chores: wash the dishes, take out the garbage, do the laundry, sweep the floor, make the bed, etc. Have students illustrate each activity and label it with the appropriate verb/noun combination.

VOCABULARY

The Kitchen	**La cuisine**	**La cocina**	**Die Küche**	**La cucina**
counter	le comptoir	el mostrador	die Theke	il banco
table	la table	la mesa	der Tisch	la tavola
microwave oven	le four à micro-ondes	el horno de microondas	der Mikrowellenherd	il forno a microonda
stove	la cuisinière	la estufa	der Herd	il fornello
oven	le four	el horno	der Backofen	il forno
refrigerator	le réfrigérateur	la nevera	der Kühlschrank	il frigorifero
freezer	le congélateur	el congelador	die Tiefkühltruhe	il congelatore
sink	l'évier	el fregadero	das Spülbecken	l'acquaio
faucet	le robinet	el grifo	der Wasserhahn	il rubinetto
dishwasher	le lave-vaisselle	el lavaplatos	die Spülmaschine	il lavapiatti
food processor	le robot	el procesador de alimentos	die Küchenmaschine	il food processor
kettle	la bouilloire	la tetera	der Wasserkessel	il bollitore
pan	la poêle	la sartén	die Pfanne	la padella
electric mixer	le batteur électrique	la batidora eléctrica	der Mixer	il miscelatore
drawer	le tiroir	el cajón	die Schublade	il cassettino
toaster	le grille-pain	el tostador	der Toaster	il tostatore
paper towels	les serviettes de papier	las toallas de papel	die Papiertücher	l'asciugamani di carta
ice cubes	les glaçons	los cubos de hielo	die Eiswürfel	i ghiacci
spatula	la spatule	la espátula	die Spachtel	la spatola
dishes	la vaisselle	los platos	das Geschirr	i piatti
chair	la chaise	la silla	der Stuhl	la sedia
apron	le tablier	el delantal	die Schürze	il grembiale
flour	la farine	la harina	das Mehl	la farina
sponge	l'éponge	la esponja	der Schwamm	la spugna

The Utility Room	**La Blanchisserie**	**El cuarto de auxilio**	**Der Abstellraum**	**La lavanderia**
washing machine	la machine à laver	la lavadora	die Waschmaschine	la lavatrice
broom	le balai	la escoba	der Besen	la scopa
vacuum cleaner	l'aspirateur	la aspiradora	Staubsauger	l'aspirapolvere
ironing board	la planche à repasser	la mesa de planchar	das Bügelbrett	la tavola da stiro
iron	le fer à repasser	la plancha	das Bügeleisen	il ferro da stiro

mop	le balai à laver	el trapeador	der Mop	la scopa di stracci
dustpan	la pelle à poussière	la pala de basura	die Kehrichtschaufel	la paletta della spazzatura
hammer	le marteau	el martillo	der Hammer	il martello
nail	le clou	el clavo	der Nagel	il chiodo
screw	la vis	el tornillo	die Schraube	la vite
screwdriver	le tournevis	el destornillador	der Schraubenzieher	il cacciavite
drill	la perceuse	el taladro	der Bohrer	il trapano
file	la lime	la lima	die Feile	la lima
toolbox	la boîte à outils	la caja de herramientas	der Werkzeugkasten	la scatola degli utensili
wrench	la clef	la llave de tuercas	der Schraubenschlüssel	la chiave
electrical outlet	la prise de courant	el enchufe	die Steckdose	la presa
brick	la brique	el ladrillo	der Backstein	il mattone
tape measure	le mètre à ruban	la cinta para medir	das Bandmaß	il metro a nastro
laundry detergent	le détergent	el detergente	das Waschmittel	il detersivo
wood	le bois	la madera	das Holz	il legno
sandpaper	le papier de verre	el papel de lija	das Sandpapier	la carta vetro
saw	la scie	la sierra	die Säge	il saracco
laundry	le linge	la ropa sucia	die Wäsche	il bucato
board	la planche	la tabla	das Brett	la tavola
flashlight	la lampe de poche	la linterna eléctrica	die Taschenlampe	la lampadina tascabile
clothes dryer	le séchoir à linge	la secadora	der Trockner	l'asciugatrice

4. The Attic

QUESTIONS ABOUT THE PICTURE

1. Name four toys in the picture.
2. Name three things you can wear.
3. Name three things on the wall or leaning against the wall.
4. Name the things in the bottom right of the picture.
5. What is the boy at the right doing?
6. What are the girls doing?
7. What is the attic like? Describe it.
8. What games in the picture have you played? What toys have you played with? What toys and games are popular with you and your friends?
9. Who do you think the couple at the bottom of the stairs are? Who do you think the children in the picture are?
10. Is it a good idea to save old things? Why do people like to save things?

ACTION STORIES

Possible topics: putting on old clothes you find in a trunk in an attic, taking a picture, cleaning up the attic

Example: Cleaning up the attic

1. Oh! The attic is a mess. Let's clean it. 2. Let's put the small toys in the trunk. 3. First, open the trunk. 4. Put the blocks and marbles in the trunk. 5. Oops! One marble rolls down the floor. 6. Pick it up and put it into the box. 7. Pick up the whistle. 8. Blow it. It still works. 9. Put it into the box. 10. We're tired! Let's clean the rest later.

GROUP ACTIVITIES

1. Classifying

Have students name as many objects from the picture as they can for each of the following categories: toys, toys for small children, games, things to wear, toys and games you can play by yourself, toys and games you can play with other children, old things you don't see anymore.

2. Guessing Game

You or a student describes the location of an object in the picture, and other students name the object being described. Have students use the equivalent of the prepositions *next to, in front of, in back of, on, in, under.*

Example: It's on the wall.

It's under the cowboy hat. *(jump rope)*

3. Chain Game

Prepare sentences that tell about activities that go with the objects in the attic. You may want to do this together with the students. Examples: We played with the toy soldiers. We played checkers. We tried on the cowboy boots. Then have students play a chain game in which each student repeats sentences previously said by other students and adds a sentence. For example, student A says, "First we looked at the photo album." Student B repeats the sentence and adds, "Next we played with the dollhouse," and so on.

4. Debate

Present the following question to students: *You can choose three things from the attic in the picture to play with. What do you choose?* Have each student write down his or her choices. Have students compare and defend their choices. At the end of the discussion, take a vote of the class to determine which three things are the most popular.

5. Role Play

Present the following role play to the students: You and a friend are in the attic. Convince him or her to play what you want to play (e.g., dress up, play checkers, play marbles, play with the dollhouse, play cowboys). You may want to supply a sample dialogue as a model or introduce expressions of persuading/suggesting, such as the equivalents of *Let's . . . , Why don't we . . . ?, It's fun to . . . .*

6. Class Project

Have students explore the question: *Are toys today different from toys in the past?* Have students interview their parents to find out what toys their parents played with. Then have them list toys popular today. In a class discussion, have them compare the lists.

WRITING

Have students do these activities independently or as whole-class or group activities.

1. List all the games in the picture that you have played. List all the toys that you have played with.
2. You are in an old house and you find a trunk in the attic. What's inside? Write about it.
3. You spent the afternoon in the attic in the picture. Tell what you did.
4. Write about your favorite toy or game.
5. Write about the two people who live in the house, the couple at the bottom of the stairs. What did the man do? What did the woman do? Who are the children? etc.

FOCUS ON LANGUAGE

Several of the activities, such as Group Activities number 3, focus on the past. Review the past tense forms of verbs with students. Focus on the verbs needed to go with the nouns in the picture: e.g., play, put on, put together, look at.

VOCABULARY

The Attic	**Le grenier**	**El desván**	**Die Dachstube**	**La soffitta**
trunk	la malle	el baúl	die Kiste	il baule
box	la boîte	la caja	die Schachtel	la scatola
dust	la poussière	el polvo	der Staub	il polvere
string	la ficelle	la cuerda	die Schnur	lo spago
cobweb	la toile d'araignée	la telaraña	die Spinnwebe	la ragnatela
ball gown	la robe de bal	el vestido de baile	das Ballkleid	il veste da ballo
top hat	le chapeau haut de forme	el sombrero de copa	der Zylinderhut	il cappello a cilindro
tuxedo	le smoking	el esmoquin	der Smoking	l'abito nero
hat	le chapeau	el sombrero	der Hut	il cappello
feather	la plume	la pluma	die Feder	la piuma
cowboy hat	le chapeau de cowboy	el sombrero de vaquero	der Cowboyhut	il cappello di cowboy
uniform	l'uniforme	el uniforme	die Uniform	la divisa
cowboy boots	les bottes de cowboy	las botas de vaquero	die Cowboystiefel	gli stivali di cowboy
photo album	l'album de photos	el álbum de fotos	das Fotoalbum	l'album di fotografie
game	le jeu	el juego	das Spiel	il gioco
doll	la poupée	la muñeca	die Puppe	la bambola
jigsaw puzzle	le puzzle	el rompecabezas	das Puzzle	il rompicapo
jump rope	la corde à sauter	la cuerda de brincar	das Springseil	la corda
teddy bear	le nounours	el osito	der Teddybär	l'orsacchiotto
toys	les jouets	los juguetes	die Spielsachen	i giocattoli
whistle	le sifflet	el pito	die Pfeife	lo zufolo
cards	les cartes	los naipes	die Karten	le carte
dice	les dés	los dados	die Würfel	i dadi
blocks	les cubes	los cubos	die Bauklötze	i blocchi
electric train	le train électrique	el tren eléctrico	der elektrische Zug	il trenino
magnet	l'aimant	el imán	der Magnet	il magnete
cradle	le berceau	la cuna	die Wiege	la culla
coloring book	le livre à colorier	el libro de colorear	das Ausmalbuch	il libro di disegni
music box	la boîte à musique	la cajita de música	die Spieldose	la scatola della musica
yarn	la laine	el hilado	das Garn	la filaccia
knitting needles	les aiguilles à tricoter	las agujas de tejer	die Stricknadeln	i ferri da calza

dollhouse	la maison de poupée	la casa de muñecas	das Puppenhaus	la casa da bambole
comic books	les livres de bandes dessinées	los libros de cómicos	die Comics	i giornali a fumetti
lightbulb	l'ampoule	la bombilla	die Glühbirne	la lampadina
toy soldiers	les soldats de plomb	los soldados de juego	die Spielzeugsoldaten	i piccoli soldati
movie projector	le projecteur	el proyector de película	der Scheinwerfer	il proiettore
umbrella	le parapluie	el paraguas	der Regenschirm	l'ombrello
puppet	la marionnette	el títere	die Handpuppe	il burrattino
fan	l'éventail	el abanico	der Fächer	il ventaglio
marbles	les billes	las canicas	die Murmeln	le palline di marmo
rocking horse	le cheval à bascule	el caballo mecedor	das Schaukelpferd	il cavallo a dondolo
chess	le jeu d'échecs	el ajedrez	das Schachspiel	il gioco degli scacchi
photograph	la photo	la fotografía	die Photographie	la foto
spinning wheel	le rouet	el torno de hilar	das Spinnrad	il filatoio
picture frame	le cadre	el marco	der Bilderrahmen	la cornice
rocking chair	la chaise à bascule	la mecedora	der Schaukelstuhl	la sedia a dondolo
checkers	le jeu de dames	el juego de damas	das Mühlespiel	il gioco della dama

5. The Four Seasons

QUESTIONS ABOUT THE PICTURES

1. In what season is it hot?
2. Name two things you see on the ground in winter.
3. Name three things that you might see when it rains.
4. Name three animals you might see in a garden in the summer.
5. What is the weather like in the spring?
6. What things do people do in their yard in each season?
7. What is the yard like in the fall?
8. Does the weather change for the seasons where you live?
9. Is the weather where you live different from the weather in the pictures?
10. What different things do you do outside in each of the seasons?

ACTION STORIES

Possible topics: being in the yard in summer, winter, etc., how to build a snowman, how to shovel snow, how to plant a garden, how to rake leaves

Example: Being in the yard in summer

1. It's summer. 2. Let's do things in the yard. 3. Get the water hose. 4. Water the plants. 5. Get the lawn mower. 6. Cut the grass. 7. You're tired. 8. Sit on the hammock. 9. Be careful! Don't fall.

GROUP ACTIVITIES

1. Classifying

Have students name as many objects from the picture as they can for each of the following categories: tools you use in the yard, things you see in the sky, animals you see in the yard, games you play in the yard, things that have to do with rain, things that are cold, things that are wet.

2. What Goes With Each Season?

Prepare (or have students prepare) several sets of index cards. Each card should have on it one of the words from the transparency. Have students work in small groups. Mix up each set of cards, and pass out one set to each group. Have students write the name of the season to which each word belongs. Note that some words (e.g., bird, flowers) may belong to more than one season. Have students try to identify all the seasons for each word. Have the groups compare their answers.

3. Chanting/Chain Game

Have individual students chant a sentence about a season, each time adding a new word to the sentence. For example: In the summer, summer, summer, in my garden, garden, garden, I see a fly, and I see a grasshopper, and I see a fan, etc.

4. Word Association

Encourage students to think of other words that relate to each of the seasons. These may vary from language to language, or place to place.

Examples:

Summer: hot, swim, bathing suit, pool, watermelon

Fall: football, cool, sweater, pumpkins

Winter: cold, ice skating, gloves

Spring: umbrella, seed, raincoat, cool

5. Debate

Present the following questions to the students: Which is your favorite season? Why did you choose it? *(you can play your favorite sport, you like snow, etc.)* Have each student write down his or her choice. Have students compare their answers and defend their choices. At the end of the discussion, take a vote to determine which season is most popular.

WRITING

Have students do these activities independently or as whole-class or group activities.

1. Draw a picture to show each of the four seasons. For each season, draw things that you see in that season. Write the words for the things you have drawn on the picture or on another sheet of paper.
2. Write a story for each season where you live. In the story, tell what the season is like. Tell what you see in each season. Tell what you do in each season.
3. Tell about what you see outside the window of the classroom or outside the window of your house right now.
4. Which of the pictures in the transparency or on the pages would you most like to be in? What would you do? Write your answers.

FOCUS ON LANGUAGE

1. Review/present sentences that relate to the weather:
   It's cold/hot/cool in winter/summer/spring.
   It rains/snows in spring/winter.
   Ask students questions such as: How is the weather in summer? Does it snow in summer?
2. Review/present the names of the months of the year. Have students identify which months go with which seasons. In the presentation, show a calendar and ask students to tell the month that is *before or after* another month you name.

VOCABULARY

The Four Seasons	**Les quatre saisons**	**Las cuatro estaciones**	**Die ver Jahreszeiten**	**Le quattro stagioni**
winter	*l'hiver*	*el invierno*	*der Winter*	*l'inverno*
snow	la neige	la nieve	der Schnee	la neve
ice	la glace	el hielo	das Eis	il ghiaccio
snowflake	le flocon de neige	el copo de nieve	die Schneeflocke	il fiocco di neve
icicle	la chandelle de glace	el carámbano	der Eiszapfen	il ghiacciolo
shovel	la pelle	la pala	die Schaufel	la pala
snowstorm	la tempête de neige	la tormenta de nieve	der Schneesturm	il turbine di neve
sled	le traîneau	el trineo	der Schlitten	la slitta
snowplow	le chasse-neige	la máquina barredora de nieve	der Schneepflug	lo spazzaneve
snowmobile	la motoneige	el carro de nieve	das Schneemobil	il gatto delle nevi
snowman	le bonhomme de neige	la figura de nieve	der Schneemann	l'uomo di neve
snowball	la boule de neige	la bola de nieve	der Schneeball	la palotta di neve
log	la bûche	el tronco	der Holzklotz	il ceppo
summer	*l'été*	*el verano*	*der Sommer*	*l'estate*
butterfly	le papillon	la mariposa	der Schmetterling	la farfalla
fly	la mouche	la mosca	die Fliege	la mosca
fly swatter	la tapette	el matamoscas	der Fliegenwedel	il chiappamosche
fan	le ventilateur	el ventilador	der Ventilator	il ventilatore
sprinkler	l'appareil d'arrosage	la regadera	der Rasensprenger	lo spruzzatore
grasshopper	la sauterelle	el saltamontes	die Heuschrecke	la cavalletta
lawn mower	la tondeuse à gazon	la cortadora de grama	der Rasenmäher	la falciatrice meccanica
barbecue	le gril	la barbacoa	der Grill	la griglia
hammock	le hamac	la hamaca	die Hängematte	i fiammiferi
yard	la cour	el patio	der Hof	il cortile
deck	le patio	el patio	die Veranda	il portico
garden hose	le tuyau d'arrosage	la manguera de jardín	der Gartenschlauch	l'idrante
matches	les allumettes	los fósforos	die Streichhölzer	l'amaca

spring	*le printemps*	*la primavera*	*der Frühling*	*la primavera*
rain	la pluie	la lluvia	der Regen	la pioggia
rainbow	l'arc-en-ciel	el arco iris	der Regenbogen	l'arcobaleno
stem	la tige	el tallo	der Stengel	lo stelo
bird	l'oiseau	el pájaro	der Vogel	l'uccello
worm	le ver	el gusano	der Wurm	il verme
raindrop	la goutte de pluie	la gota de lluvia	der Regentropfen	la goccia di pioggia
flowers	les fleurs	las flores	die Blumen	i fiori
flowerbed	le parterre	el cuadro de jardín	das Blumenbeet	l'aiuola
petal	le pétale	el pétalo	das Blütenblatt	il petalo
vegetable garden	le jardin potager	la hortaliza	der Gemüsegarten	l'orto
lightning	l'éclair	el relámpago	der Blitz	il fulmine
fall	*l'automne*	*el otoño*	*der Herbst*	*l'autunno*
wind	le vent	el viento	der Wind	il vento
leaf	la feuille	la hoja	das Blatt	la foglia
branch	la branche	la rama	der Zweig	il ramo
fog	le brouillard	la niebla	der Nebel	la nebbia
rake	le râteau	el rastrillo	der Rechen	il rastrello
clouds	les nuages	las nubes	die Wolken	le nuvole
kite	le cerf-volant	la cometa	der Drachen	l'aquilone
puddle	la flaque d'eau	el charco	die Pfütze	la pozzanghera
mud	la boue	el lodo	der Matsch	il fango
bird's nest	le nid d'oiseau	el nido de pájaro	das Vogelnest	il nido
bush	le buisson	el arbusto	der Busch	il cespuglio

6. At the Supermarket

QUESTIONS ABOUT THE PICTURE

1. Name two things in which you put groceries.
2. Name things you can drink.
3. Name things you put into a salad.
4. What are some things you eat for dessert/for snacks?
5. What things are in the man's cart *(at left)*/on the checkout counter?
6. What things are dairy products?
7. What are the names of some of the departments in a supermarket? *(meat, fish, frozen food, fruits and vegetables/produce, canned food, deli, etc.)*
8. What other kinds of things can you buy in some supermarkets? *(e.g., film, medicines, greeting cards, etc.)*
9. Where do you and your family go to buy groceries?
10. Why do people like to go to large stores?

ACTION STORIES

Possible topics: buying groceries (going through the store with a cart), choosing fruit, checking out

Example: Buying groceries

1. Get a shopping cart. 2. Push your cart down the aisle. 3. Let's get some bread. 4. Take a loaf of bread from the shelf. 5. Put the loaf into your cart. 6. Now get a carton of milk and put it into your cart. 7. Push your cart to the fruit and vegetable counter. 8. Put a bunch of bananas into your cart. 9. That's all we need. Now push your cart to the checkout counter. 10. Put your groceries on the checkout counter. 11. Watch the cashier ring up the prices on the cash register. 12. Give the cashier the money for the groceries.

GROUP ACTIVITIES

1. Classifying

Have students name as many objects from the picture as they can for each of the following categories: vegetables, fruits, things to eat for breakfast, things you buy by weight, green vegetables, things you eat with bread, things you eat for dessert, what you see at the checkout counter.

2. Organize the Store

Prepare (or have students prepare) several sets of index cards. Each card should have on it one of the words from the scene. Have students work in small groups. Mix up each set of cards, and pass out one set to each group. Tell students that their task is to organize the store. These are the departments/places: vegetable area, fruit area, dairy products, snacks, desserts, checkout area, bakery, meat, frozen food. Students should prepare a sheet of paper with the name of each of the places. They are to put each of the word cards on the appropriate sheet. Have groups compare their answers.

3. Chanting

Prepare sentences that tell what you eat for different meals. You may want to do this together with the students.

Examples:

For breakfast, I have toast and cereal.

For lunch, I have milk and fruit.

For dinner, I have a frozen dinner and pie.

Using appropriate sentences, make up chants (in which key words are repeated) for students to perform.

Example: For breakfast, breakfast, breakfast, I have toast, toast, toast, and cereal, cereal, cereal.

4. Role Play

Set up a store with the students. Prepare cards with food names (and pictures on them if possible). Students are to buy what they want to eat for dinner. Students should choose the food (cards) they want and check out with the "cashier." Both the "buyer" and the "cashier" should say what is being bought.

For more advanced students, add prices for the food items (by weight, by box). Give each student "shopper" a certain amount of "money." Students must be careful not to choose more items than they can pay for. The "cashier" should check that the "buyers" have spent less than the limit. If practical, the cashier should say the prices of the selected items and total the cost on a calculator.

5. Discussion

Have students talk about places in the neighborhood in which they can buy food. Topics to cover: What kind of food/products can you buy in each? Are there differences in prices? Which stores are more convenient/easier to shop in?

WRITING

Have students do these activities independently or as whole-class or group activities.

1. You are buying dinner for your family tonight. Write a shopping list. Write what you want to buy.
2. Make two lists: write the names of food you really like and the names of food you don't like.
3. Make two lists: write the names of food you eat often and the names of food you don't eat often.
4. Write an ad for the supermarket. Be sure to list special items and special prices that the supermarket is offering.

FOCUS ON LANGUAGE

Review/present the basic words used to describe weight in the target language (e.g., pound, ounces, kilogram, 100 grams, liter). Bring in boxes and cans of food in the various weights. Give students hands-on experience in feeling the weight of the objects and reading the measurements on the labels.

VOCABULARY

At the Supermarket	Au supermarché	En el supermercado	Im Supermarkt	Al supermercato
vegetables	les légumes	las legumbres	das Gemüse	gli ortaggi
cabbage	le chou	la col	das Kraut	il cavolo
lettuce	la laitue	la lechuga	der Salat	la lattuga
green beans	les haricots verts	las judías verdes	die grünen Bohnen	i fagiolini
peas	les petits pois	los guisantes	die Erbsen	i piselli
carrots	les carottes	las zanahorias	die Karotten	le carote
tomatoes	les tomates	los tomates	die Tomaten	i pomodori
potatoes	les pommes de terre	las papas	die Kartoffeln	le patate
onions	les oignons	las cebollas	die Zwiebeln	le cipolle
spinach	les épinards	las espinacas	der Spinat	gli spinaci
avocado	l'avocat	el aguacate	die Avokado	l'avocado
nuts	les noix	las nueces	die Nüsse	le noci
chocolate	le chocolat	el chocolate	die Schokolade	la cioccolata
candy	les bonbons	los dulces	die Süßigkeiten	le caramelle
pie	la tarte	la empanada	der Obstkuchen	la torta
fruit	les fruits	la fruta	das Obst	le frutta
apple	la pomme	la manzana	der Apfel	la mela
orange	l'orange	la naranja	die Orange	l'arancia
lemon	le citron	el limón	die Zitrone	il limone
lime	le citron vert	el limón verde	die Limone	il tiglio
cherries	les cerises	las cerezas	die Kirsche	le ciliege
banana	la banane	el plátano	die Banane	la banana
grapes	les raisins	las uvas	die Trauben	le uva
strawberries	les fraises	las fresas	die Erdbeeren	le fragole
peach	la pêche	el durazno	der Pfirsich	la pesca
grapefruit	le pamplemousse	la toronja	die Pampelmuse	il pompelmo
melon	le melon	el melón	die Melone	il melone
watermelon	la pastèque	la sandía	die Wassermelone	il cocomero
raspberries	les framboises	las frambuesas	die Himbeeren	i lamponi
pineapple	l'ananas	la piña	die Ananas	l'ananas
meat	la viande	la carne	das Fleisch	la carne

eggs	les œufs	los huevos	die Eier	le uova
butter	le beurre	la mantequilla	die Butter	il burro
bread	le pain	el queso	das Brot	il pane
cheese	le fromage	el pan	der Käse	il formaggio
food	la nourriture	la comida	das Essen	il cibo
milk	le lait	la leche	die Milch	il latte
cookies	les petits gâteaux	las galletas dulces	die Plätzchen	i biscotti
crackers	les biscuits salés	las galletas	die Kekse	i crackers
potato chips	les chips	las papas fritas a la inglesa	die Kartoffelchips	le patatine
bottle	la bouteille	la botella	die Flasche	la bottiglia
fruit juice	le jus de fruit	el jugo	der Fruchtsaft	il succo
cereal	les céréales	el cereal	die Cornflakes	i cereali
can	la boîte de conserve	la lata	die Dose	la scatola
frozen dinner	le plat surgelé	la cena congelada	die Tiefkühlkost	il pranzo surgelato
soap	le savon	el jabón	die Seife	il sapone
money	l'argent	el dinero	das Geld	il denaro
shopping cart	le chariot	el carrito de compras	der Einkaufswagen	il carrello
shopping bag	le sac à provisions	la bolsa de compras	die Tüte	il pacco per la spesa
sign	l'affiche	el letrero	das Zeichen	il cartellino
scale	la balance	la báscula	die Waage	la bilancia
price	le prix	el precio	der Preis	il prezzo
cash register	la caisse	la caja	die Kasse	la cassa
cashier	la caissière	la cajera	die Kassiererin	la cassiere

7. Clothes

QUESTIONS ABOUT THE PICTURE

1. Name things you can wear to bed.
2. Name things you might wear when it rains.
3. Name things you wear in hot/cold weather.
4. Name the jewelry in the picture.
5. Name two things on clothes that you can open and close.
6. What do you usually wear to school?
7. What is your favorite outfit?
8. Where do people go to buy clothes?
9. Singers and movie stars often wear clothes that are unusual. Can you think of some examples of people who do so?
10. What kinds of clothes are popular with students your age?

ACTION STORIES

Possible topics: getting dressed, getting ready to go outside in cold weather *(gloves, earmuffs, down vest, coat),* getting ready to go outside when it might be raining *(umbrella, raincoat, boots),* packing a suitcase, buying clothes in a store

Example: Getting dressed

1. It's morning and it's time to get dressed. 2. Put on your shirt or blouse. 3. Button it up. 4. Now put on your pants. 5. Zip them up. 6. Sit down. 7. Put on your socks—left foot, right foot. 8. Put on your shoes—left foot, right foot. 9. You're ready to go!

GROUP ACTIVITIES

1. Classifying

Have students name as many objects from the picture as they can for each of the following categories: things you wear on your head, things you wear on your feet, things you wear on your legs, clothing for winter, clothing for bed, things boys wear, things girls wear, things you wear on your waist, things you wear above your waist, things you wear below your waist.

2. Chanting

Prepare sentences that tell what you can wear on different parts of the body. You may want to do this together with the students.

Examples:

I wear a hat on my head.

I wear socks on my feet.

I wear pants on my legs.

I wear glasses on my nose.

Using appropriate sentences, make up chants (in which key words are repeated) for students to perform.

Example: I wear a hat, hat, hat on my head, head, head.

3. Debate

You can choose eight pieces of clothing to take with you on a trip to a cold place. What do you take? Have each student write down his or her choices. Have students compare and defend their choices. Then have students do the same activity, this time for a trip to a hot place.

4. Role Play

Set up a department store in your classroom. Make signs to indicate the various departments: children's clothes, shoes, coats, hats. Put pictures of various pieces of clothing in the appropriate departments or, if possible, use real clothing items. Model a sample dialogue between a salesperson and a customer. Then present the language for the salesperson: *May I help you? Here is/are the . . . How does it fit? Do you want to take it?* Present the language for the customer: *I'd like to see a . . . May I try it on? It's too big/too small. It fits. I'll buy it.* Have students role-play being salespeople and customers.

WRITING

Have students do these activities independently or as whole-class or group activities.

1. List what you are wearing now.
2. *(Cut pictures of people from magazines for this activity.)* List what the person is wearing.

3. Pretend you are a dress designer. Design an outfit. Decide on a place to wear it: to the beach, to play a sport, go to a concert. Label the parts of the outfit.
4. Draw a picture of a clothing store. Show a number of departments: children's, women's, men's. Label what you would find in each department.
5. Invent a magic piece of clothing. It might be glasses that let you see for more than a mile, a coat that makes you invisible, shoes that let you fly, or a hat that makes you smart. Write a story about what happens when you or a character wear that piece of clothing.

FOCUS ON LANGUAGE

1. Review/present the verbs for *putting on/taking off/wearing* pieces of clothing. Present the verbs by demonstrating with a hat, glove, etc. Then have students perform the actions.
2. Review/present the parts of the body. You can do this by pointing to parts of the body and having students name the parts.

VOCABULARY

Clothing	Les vêtements	La ropa	Die Kleidung	Abiti
glasses	les lunettes	los anteojos	die Brille	gli occhiali
underwear	les sous-vêtements	la ropa interior	die Unterwäsche	la biancheria intima
buckle	la boucle	la hebilla	die Schnalle	la fibbia
belt	la ceinture	el cinturón	der Gürtel	la cintura
pants	le pantalon	los pantalones	die Hosen	i pantaloni
collar	le col	el cuello	der Kragen	il collo
blouse	le chemisier	la blusa	die Bluse	la camicetta
bracelet	le bracelet	la pulsera	das Armband	il braccialetto
skirt	la jupe	la falda	der Rock	la gonna
shoes	les chaussures	los zapatos	die Schuhe	le scarpe
socks	les chaussettes	los calcetines	die Socken	i calzini
ring	la bague	la sortija	der Ring	l'anello
hat	le chapeau	el sombrero	der Hut	il cappello
sunglasses	les lunettes noires	los anteojos de sol	die Sonnenbrille	gli occhiali scuri
earring	la boucle d'oreille	el arete	der Ohrring	l'orecchino
shorts	le short	los pantalones cortos	die Shorts	i calzoncini corti
sandals	les sandales	las sandalias	die Sandalen	i sandali
sweatshirt	le sweat-shirt	la camisa de entrenamiento	das Sweatshirt	la maglietta sportiva
sweatpants	le pantalon de survêtement	los pantalones de entrenamiento	die Trainingshosen	i pantaloni della tuta
hood	le capuchon	la capucha	die Kapuze	il cappuccio
raincoat	l'imperméable	el impermeable	der Regenmantel	l'impermeabile
zipper	la fermeture éclair	la cremallera	der Reißverschluß	la cerniera
pocket	la poche	el bolsillo	die Tasche	la tasca
shirt	la chemise	la camisa	das Hemd	la camicia
tie	la cravate	la corbata	die Krawatte	la cravatta
sleeve	la manche	la manga	der Ärmel	la manica
suit	le complet	el traje	der Anzug	il completo
necklace	le collier	el collar	die Halskette	la collana
dress	la robe	el vestido	das Kleid	il vestito
bathing suit	le maillot de bain	el traje de baño	der Badeanzug	il costume da bagno

backpack	le sac à dos	la mochila	der Rucksack	lo zaino
T-shirt	le teeshirt	la camiseta	das Unterhemd	la maglietta
watch	la montre	el reloj	die Uhr	l'orologio
umbrella	le parapluie	el paraguas	der Regenschirm	l'ombrello
boots	les bottes	las botas	die Stiefel	gli stivali
sweater	le pullover	el suéter	der Pullover	il golf
gym shoes	les chaussures de gymnastique	los zapatos de tenis	die Turnschuhe	le scarpe da tennis
shoelace	le lacet	el cordón	die Schuhsenkel	la stringa
earmuffs	les serre-tête	las orejeras	die Ohrenklappen	il paraorecchie
button	le bouton	el botón	der Knopf	il bottone
handkerchief	le mouchoir	el pañuelo	das Taschentuch	il fazzoletto
coat	le manteau	el abrigo	der Mantel	il cappotto
gloves	les gants	los guantes	die Handschuhe	i guanti
tights	les collants	el traje de malla	die Strumpfhose	la calzamaglia
down vest	le gilet de duvet	el chaleco de plumón	die Daunenweste	il gilè di piuma
jeans	les jeans	los vaqueros	die Jeans	i jeans
hiking boots	les chaussures d'excursion	las botas de campo	die Wanderstiefel	gli scarponi
scarf	l'écharpe	la bufanda	das Halstuch	la sciarpa
jacket	le blouson	la chaqueta	die Jacke	la giacca
mittens	les moufles	las manoplas	die Fäustlinge	i guanti a manopola
bathrobe	le peignoir	la bata	der Bademantel	l'accappatoio
pajamas	le pyjama	el pijama	der Schlafanzug	la pigiama
cap	le bonnet de ski	el gorro	die Strickmütze	il cappello da sci

8. In the City

QUESTIONS ABOUT THE PICTURE

1. Name three kinds of stores.
2. Name three things in the playground.
3. Name four things that have to do with cars.
4. What things are along the beach?
5. Name some of the things that the people in the picture are doing.
6. What kinds of things can you buy in a clothing store, pharmacy, etc.?
7. What things in the playground have you played on?
8. What things might you see in a museum?
9. How tall was the tallest building you have been in?
10. How is your town or city different from the one in the picture?

ACTION STORIES

Possible topics: how to slide down a slide, how to get to a certain place, how to buy something in a store

Example: How to get to the train station (from the pharmacy)

1. We're in front of the pharmacy. Let's go to the train station. 2. Walk straight ahead to the corner. 3. Turn right. 4. Walk straight ahead to the next corner. 5. Cross the street. 6. Now turn left. 7. Walk past the fire hydrant. 8. Walk past the park. 9. Walk to the stairs of the train station. 10. Walk up the stairs. 11. It's three o'clock. 12. Run! Our train leaves in two minutes!

GROUP ACTIVITIES

1. Classifying

Have students name as many objects from the picture as they can for each of the following categories: things in the park, things in the playground, stores, kinds of buildings, things on the street, parts of buildings.

2. Guessing Game

You or a student describes the location of an object in the picture, and other students name the object being described. Have students use the equivalent of the phrases *next to, on the same street as, across the street from, between, on, in.*

Example: It's between the pharmacy and the restaurant. *(the movie theater)*

3. Vocabulary Extension/Review

Have students discuss the kinds of things that they can buy in each of the stores. This activity ties in with these units: 4 The Attic (for toys), 6 At the Supermarket (for grocery items), 7 Clothing, 10 In a Restaurant, 11 The Doctor's Office (for pharmacy items). You might want to prompt with additional vocabulary for the bakery and butcher shop. If students are familiar with the words, have them draw and list the items that they can buy in each of the stores. Also, have them role-play buying items in the stores, using the language they practiced in the role plays in units 7 and 10, for ordering or buying things in a store.

4. Debate

You can visit three places in the picture. What do you want to visit? Have each student write down his or her choices. Have students compare and defend their choices. At the end of the discussion, take a vote to determine the most popular places.

5. Role Play/Interview

Have individual students take the following roles:

a. *You are the mayor of the city in the picture. Tell why you think your city is a great place to live.* The rest of the class is to ask questions about such things as the kinds of stores, places people can go to relax, etc. To facilitate the activity, depending on level of the students, you might want to take the role of mayor first to act as a model of things that can be said.

b. You are a tour guide for the city in the picture. Prepare a speech telling about places (e.g., what you can see in the museum, the person in the statue in the park, etc.).

WRITING

Have students do these activities independently or as whole-class or group activities.

1. List all the things from the picture that you can see in your own city or town.
2. List all the things that you like to do in your playground or park.
3. You are on the top of the skyscraper at the top right of the picture. Describe what you can see.
4. Design a new town. Draw a picture of it. Label each of the buildings.
5. Make an ad for one of the stores in the picture. Be sure to tell about the kinds of things you can buy in the store.

FOCUS ON LANGUAGE

In connection with the Action Stories, review/present the vocabulary for giving directions: for example, the equivalent of *turn, left, right, straight ahead, at the traffic lights, at the next corner,* etc.

VOCABULARY

In the City	En ville	En la ciudad	In die Stadt	Nella città
building	le bâtiment	el edificio	das Gebäude	l'edificio
skyscraper	le gratte-ciel	el rascacielos	der Wolkenkratzer	il grattacielo
factory	l'usine	la fábrica	die Fabrik	la fabbrica
smokestack	la cheminée	la chimenea	der Schornstein	il fumaiolo
traffic lights	les feux de circulation	el semáforo	die Verkehrsampel	il semaforo
manhole cover	la plaque d'égout	la tapa de registro	der Kanaldeckel	la bocca di accesso
driveway	l'entrée	el camino particular	die Auffahrt	la strada privata
parking lot	le parc de stationnement	el aparcamiento	der Parkplatz	il parcheggio
parking meter	le parcomètre	el parquímetro	die Parkuhr	il parchimetro
corner	le coin	la esquina	die Ecke	l'angolo
fire hydrant	la bouche d'incendie	la boca de incendios	der Hydrant	l'idrante
square	la place	la plaza	der Platz	la piazza
statue	la statue	la estatua	die Statue	la statua
apartment building	l'immeuble	el edificio de apartamentos	das Wohnhaus	l'edificio degli appartamenti
fire escape	l'escalier de secours	la escalera de incendios	die Rettungsleiter	la scala di sicurezza
balcony	le balcon	el balcón	der Balkon	il balcone
fire station	la caserne de pompiers	la estación de bomberos	die Feuerwehrwache	la stazione dei pompieri
police station	la gendarmerie	la estación de policía	die Polizeiwache	il posto di polizia
jail	la prison	la cárcel	das Gefängnis	il carcere
bookstore	la librairie	la librería	die Buchhandlung	la libreria
toy store	le magasin de jouets	la juguetería	der Spielwarenladen	il negozio dei gioccattoli
grocery store	l'épicerie	la tienda de comestibles	der Laden	la drogheria
bakery	la boulangerie	la pastelería	die Bäckerei	la panetteria
butcher shop	la boucherie	la carnicería	die Metzgerei	la macelleria
fountain	la fontaine	la fuente	der Brunnen	la fontana
newspaper	le journal	el periódico	die Zeitung	il giornale
train station	la gare	la estación del tren	der Bahnhof	la stazione
church	l'église	la iglesia	die Kirche	la chiesa
school	l'école	la escuela	die Schule	la scuola
museum	le musée	el museo	das Museum	il museo
hospital	l'hôpital	el hospital	das Krankenhaus	l'ospedale

drugstore (pharmacy)	la pharmacie	la farmacia	die Apotheke	la farmacia
movie theater	le cinéma	el cine	das Kino	il cinema
restaurant	le restaurant	el restaurante	das Restaurant	il ristorante
clothing store	le magasin de vêtements	el almacén	der Bekleidungsladen	il negozio di confezioni
hotel	l'hôtel	el hotel	das Hotel	l'albergo
traffic jam	l'embouteillage	el embotellamiento de tráfico	der Verkehrsstau	l'intasamento
crane	la grue	la grúa	der Kran	la gru
bench	le banc	el banco	die Bank	la panca
sign	l'affiche	la señal	das Zeichen	il segno
playground	le terrain de jeux	el patio de recreo	der Spielplatz	il parco giochi
park	le parc	el parque	der Park	il parco
jungle gym	le jungle-gym	las barras	das Spielgerät	l'attrezzo ginnico
swings	les balançoires	los columpios	die Schaukel	l'altalena
seesaw	la balançoire	el sube y baja	die Wippe	il su in giù
slide	le toboggan	el tobogán	die Rutschbahn	la scivola
sandbox	le tas de sable	el cajón de arena	der Sandkasten	il recinto con sabbia
beach	la plage	la playa	der Strand	la spiaggia

9. In the Country

QUESTIONS ABOUT THE PICTURE

1. Name two buildings on the farm.
2. Name six animals you see on a farm.
3. Name two things that have to do with camping.
4. Name the people in the picture.
5. What is the farmer doing?
6. Tell about what the people at the left are doing.
7. *(left, center)* What problem is the man with the hat having?
8. *(left)* Why does the woman with the baby look surprised?
9. What farm animals would you like as pets?
10. Have you ever been on a farm? What did you see or do there?

ACTION STORIES

Possible topics: having a picnic, walking around a farm *(go into the barn, pet the horses, go outside to the yard, feed the chickens, go to the fence, look at the pigs)*

> *Example:* Having a picnic
>
> 1. Let's get ready for our picnic. 2. Put the blanket on the ground. 3. Open the picnic basket. 4. Take out the dishes and glasses. 5. Put them on the tablecloth. 6. Take out the sandwiches. 7. Take out the grapes. 8. Let's eat! 9. Oops! We forgot the napkins. 10. Look in the picnic basket and take them out.

GROUP ACTIVITIES

1. Classifying

Have students name as many objects from the picture as they can for each of the following categories: animals, baby animals, birds, insects, animals that can be pets, animals with horns, people in the picture, buildings on the farm, things that have to do with the train.

2. Barnyard Mixup

Tell students the following story:

> All the doors in the barns were left open, and the gates in the fences were left open, too. Now all the animals are in the wrong places. We need to put all the animals of the same kind together.

Put the following list on the board or a transparency:

1	**2**	**3**	**4**	**5**
rooster	cow	gosling	puppy	horse
pig	colt	kitten	goat	bull
dog	duck			

6	**7**	**8**	**9**	**10**
hen	colt	goose	sheep	duckling
piglet	chick	cat	calf	kid

Then have students regroup the words into animal families. If students have word cards, they can group them as listed below and rearrange them. For more advanced classes, you can complicate the task: List only two animals for the first two groups. Tell students that two animals are missing and their task is to match up the animals and then identify the missing animals.

3. Song

Prepare a song based on "Old Mac Donald Had a Farm," using the names of the animals in the picture and supplying the sounds that the animals make, as described in the target language. Teach the song to the class.

4. Memory Game

Have students work in pairs or small groups. They are not to look at the picture. Have them write down the names of (or draw) as many objects from the farm as they can remember from the picture. Have groups compare their answers.

5. Debate

Is it better to live in the city or the country? With the class, discuss what is good about each place. Have students decide on the place they prefer. In a class discussion, have students tell why they made their choice.

WRITING

Have students do these activities independently or as whole-class or group activities.

1. List the things/animals you would most like to see on a farm.
2. List all the animals in the picture that you have seen.
3. You are on the train that is going to pass the farm. Describe what you see as you pass the farm.
4. Describe a time that you had a picnic or went camping. Did you have any problems, like ants or rain?
5. Write about the picture in the unit. Write as many sentences as you can to explain what is in it.

FOCUS ON LANGUAGE

Each language has idioms that contain the names of animals. Often lists of these can be found in idiom books. Present some of the idioms to the class. For example, in English, some idioms with animals are *raining cats and dogs, as quiet as a mouse, eat like a pig, get up with the chickens, as busy as a bee.* You might have students draw pictures to illustrate the idioms.

VOCABULARY

In the Country	À la campagne	En el campo	Auf dem Land	In paese
farmer	le fermier	el granjero	der Bauer	l'agricoltore
tractor	le tracteur	el tractor	der Traktor	il trattore
barn	la grange	el granero	die Scheune	il granaio
hay	le foin	la paja	das Heu	il fieno
dog	le chien	el perro	der Hund	il cane
puppy	le chiot	el cachorro	das Hündchen	il cucciolo
cat	le chat	el gato	die Katze	il gatto
kitten	le chaton	el gatito	das Kätzchen	il gattino
rooster	le coq	el gallo	der Hahn	il gallo
hen	la poule	la gallina	das Huhn	la gallina
chick	le poussin	el pollito	das Hühnchen	il pulcino
pig	le cochon	el cerdo	das Schwein	il maiale
piglet	le porcelet	el cochinillo	das Schweinchen	il porcellino
rabbit	le lapin	el conejo	der Hase	il coniglio
bull	le taureau	el toro	der Bulle	il toro
cow	la vache	la vaca	die Kuh	la mucca
calf	le veau	el becerro	das Kalb	il vitello
horse	le cheval	el caballo	das Pferd	il cavallo
colt	le poulain	el potro	das Fohlen	il puledro
duck	le canard	el pato	die Ente	l'anitra
duckling	le caneton	el patito	das Entchen	l'anatroccolo
goat	la chèvre	la cabra	die Ziege	la capra
kid	le chevreau	el chivato	das Zicklein	il capretto
goose	l'oie	el ganso	die Gans	l'oca
gosling	l'oison	el gansarón	das Gänslein	il papero
sheep	le mouton	la oveja	das Schaf	la pecora
lamb	l'agneau	el cordero	das Lamm	l'agnello
mouse	la souris	el ratón	die Maus	il topo
horns	les cornes	los cuernos	die Hörner	le corna
donkey	l'âne	el burro	der Esel	l'asino
bees	les abeilles	las abejas	die Bienen	le api

frog	la grenouille	la rana	der Frosch	la rana
pond	l'étang	el estanque	der Teich	lo stagno
grass	l'herbe	la hierba	das Gras	l'erba
fence	la clôture	la cerca	der Zaun	il recinto
tree	l'arbre	el árbol	der Baum	l'albero
shadow	l'ombre	la sombra	der Schatten	l'ombra
hill	la colline	la colina	der Hügel	la collina
road	la route	el camino	der Weg	la strada
smoke	la fumée	el humo	der Rauch	il fumo
picnic	le pique-nique	la excursión	das Picknick	il picnic
ant	la fourmi	la hormiga	die Ameise	la formica
dirt	la terre	la tierra	der Schmutz	la terra
tent	la tente	la tienda de campaña	das Zelt	la tenda
sky	le ciel	el cielo	der Himmel	il cielo
train tracks	la voie ferrée	las vías de ferrocarril	die Gleise	le rotaie
sleeping bag	le sac de couchage	el saco de dormir	der Schlafsack	il sacco a pelo
man	l'homme	el hombre	der Mann	l'uomo
woman	la femme	la mujer	die Frau	la donna
boy	le garçon	el niño	der Junge	il ragazzo
girl	la fille	la niña	das Mädchen	la ragazza
baby	le bébé	el bebé	das Baby	il piccino
farm	la ferme	la granja	der Bauernhof	la fattoria

10. In a Restaurant

QUESTIONS ABOUT THE PICTURE

1. Name the three meals of the day.
2. Name the tools you use to eat.
3. Name the people who work in a restaurant.
4. Name all the food on the tray at the right/left.
5. *(upper right/left)* What are the people at the table doing? What are they going to do next?
6. What problems are happening at the table in the center?
7. What do you eat for breakfast?
8. What foods do people eat for dessert?
9. What foods are healthful? Which foods is it better not to eat too much of?
10. Do you like restaurants like the one in the picture? Do you prefer fast-food restaurants? What are the differences between the two kinds of restaurants?

ACTION STORIES

Possible topics: eating a hamburger and fries, getting a birthday cake, serving food in a restaurant (acting as a waiter/waitress)

Example: Eating a hamburger and fries

1. Let's go to a restaurant. Sit down. 2. Let's look at the menu. 3. Let's order. Say "I'd like a hamburger and fries." 4. Here's the food. Put your napkin on your lap. 5. Put some ketchup on the hamburger. 6. Pick up your fork. 7. Use it to pick up a fry. 8. Eat it and put down the fork. 9. Then pick up your hamburger. 10. Take a bite. It tastes great!

GROUP ACTIVITIES

1. Classifying

Have students name as many objects from the picture as they can for each of the following categories: things to eat for breakfast, meat, vegetables, desserts, things people put in coffee, tools you use to eat, things you put food on, things you put on food to give it more flavor, things to do with birthdays.

2. Role Play

Have students role-play ordering food in a restaurant. One student takes the role of a waiter/waitress. You might want to take the role of the waiter/waitress at first to provide students with a model of what to say, for example, *What would you like to eat? Do you want anything to drink? Anything for dessert?* If the class or individual students have done activity 1 in the Writing section, the menu can be used in this activity.

3. Discussion

a. With the students, discuss foods that are popular in the countries in which the target language is spoken. If possible, bring in a typical menu, and have students repeat the role play of ordering in a restaurant with the menu from the country.

b. With the students, discuss birthdays, focusing on things that students usually eat at birthday parties or what children do at birthday parties in restaurants. Then present ''Happy Birthday'' in the target language and have students learn the song.

WRITING

Have students do these activities independently or as whole-class or group activities.

1. Write a menu for the restaurant in the picture. Try to include prices. You may want to divide your menu into Breakfast Food/Drinks/Main Courses/Side Dishes.
2. List your favorite foods to order when you go to a restaurant.
3. Design a menu for your own restaurant. Does it have special kinds of food? Does it have foods from different countries?
4. You are helping to organize a party at a restaurant for a friend or a fictional character. What kinds of food would be good for the meal? What food would be good for dessert?

FOCUS ON LANGUAGE

Present/review the language of ordering in a restaurant, which consists of polite requests: *I'd like . . . , please bring me . . . , may I have (more) . . . ?*

VOCABULARY

In a Restaurant	**Au restaurant**	**En un restaurante**	**Im Restaurant**	**Al ristorante**
breakfast	le petit déjeuner	el desayuno	das Frühstück	la colazione
yolk	le jaune d'œuf	la yema	das Eigelb	il rosso d'uovo
omelet	l'omelette	la tortilla	das Omelett	la frittata
toast	le pain grillé	la tostada	der Toast	il crostino
jam	la confiture	la mermelada	die Konfitüre	la marmellata
sausages	les saucissons	las salchichas	die Würste	le salsiccie
coffee	le café	el café	der Kaffee	il caffè
tea	le thé	el té	der Tee	il tè
cream	la crème	la crema	die Sahne	la panna
sugar	le sucre	el azúcar	der Zucker	lo zucchero
meals	les repas	las comidas	die Mahlzeiten	i pasti
waiter	le serveur	el camarero	der Kellner	il cameriere
waitress	la serveuse	la camarera	die Kellnerin	la cameriera
gift	le cadeau	el regalo	das Geschenk	il regalo
lunch	le déjeuner	el almuerzo	das Mittagessen	il pranzo
hamburger	le hamburger	la hamburguesa	der Hamburger	la svizzera
sandwich	le sandwich	el bocadillo	das Butterbrot	il tramezzino
french fries	les frites	las papas fritas	die Pommes frites	le patatine fritte
soup	le potage	la sopa	die Suppe	la zuppa
noodles	les nouilles	los fideos	die Nudeln	la pasta
ketchup	le ketchup	la salsa de tomate	der Ketchup	il ketchup
mustard	la moutarde	la mostaza	der Senf	la mostarda
salt	le sel	la sal	das Salz	il sale
pepper	le poivre	la pimienta	der Pfeffer	il pepe
ice cream	la glace	el helado	das Eis	il gelato
candle	la bougie	la vela	die Kerze	la candela
cake	le gâteau	la tarta	der Kuchen	la torta
birthday party	la fête d'anniversaire	la fiesta de cumpleaños	die Geburtstagsfeier	la festa di compleanno
dinner	le dîner	la cena	das Abendessen	la cena
steak	le bifteck	el bistec	das Steak	la bistecca
fish	le poisson	el pescado	der Fisch	il pesce

ham	le jambon	el jamón	der Schinken	il prosciutto
chicken	le poulet	el pollo	das Hühnerfleisch	il pollo
broccoli	le brocoli	el bróculi	die Brokkoli	i broccoletti
celery	le céleri	el apio	der Sellerie	il sedano
salad	la salade	la ensalada	der Salat	l'insalata
rice	le riz	el arroz	der Reis	il riso
mushroom	le champignon	el hongo	der Pilz	il fungo
tray	le plateau	la bandeja	das Tablett	il vassoio
tablecloth	la nappe	el mantel	die Tischdecke	la tovaglia
straw	la paille	la paja	der Trinkhalm	la cannuccia
soft drink	la boisson gazeuse	el refresco	die Limonade	la bevanda
knife	le couteau	el cuchillo	das Messer	il coltello
fork	la fourchette	el tenedor	die Gabel	la forchetta
spoon	la cuillère	la cuchara	der Löffel	il cucchiaio
plate	l'assiette	el plato	der Teller	il piatto
saucer	la soucoupe	el platillo	die Untertasse	il piattino
cup	la tasse	la taza	die Tasse	la tazza
glass	le verre	el vaso	das Glas	il bicchiere
bowl	le bol	el tazón	die Schüssel	la scodella
napkin	la serviette	la servilleta	die Serviette	il tovagliolo
menu	la carte	el menú	die Speisekarte	il menù

11. The Doctor's Office/The Dentist's Office

QUESTIONS ABOUT THE PICTURES

1. Name the people you find in the doctor's/dentist's office.
2. What is on the wall of the doctor's office?
3. *(doctor's office)* What is wrong with the boy on the examining table?
4. *(doctor's office—front left)* Name the things on the tray.
5. *(doctor's office—front right)* What is the nurse doing?
6. Name the parts of the face.
7. *(dentist's office—waiting room)* What is the little boy doing?
8. What do people usually do in the waiting room?
9. What are X rays, braces, dental floss, etc. used for?
10. Tell about your visits to the doctor's or dentist's office.

ACTION STORIES

Possible topics: locating parts of the body (e.g, *touch your mouth, touch your chin),* brushing your teeth, falling on your knee and putting on a bandage, waiting in a waiting room

Example: Brushing your teeth

1. Go to the medicine cabinet. 2. Take out your toothbrush. 3. Take out your toothpaste. 4. Open the cap on the toothpaste. 5. Squeeze some toothpaste onto the toothbrush. 6. Brush your teeth. 7. Brush up and down. 8. Be sure to brush the back teeth!

GROUP ACTIVITIES

1. Classifying

Have students name as many objects from the picture as they can for each of the following categories: parts of the leg and foot, parts of the body below your shoulder, parts of the head, things you use to clean your teeth, people in a doctor's office, people in a dentist's office, things you take when you are sick, things that are used to protect your sores/wounds, things you use to help you walk.

2. Chanting

With students, prepare sentences describing the parts of the body. Have students chant the sentences. Examples: My elbow is on my arm. My chin is under my mouth. My chest is under my shoulders. Example chant: My elbow, elbow, elbow is on my arm, arm, arm.

3. Problems/Cures

Have students work in pairs to do an information-gap activity. Prepare two sheets with problems and cures. The information that you put on one sheet should be missing from the other. Here is the complete information to appear on the two sheets:

Cures/Help	Problems
cast	broken arm/leg
sling	broken arm
bandage	cut
pills/medicine	flu
braces	crooked teeth
X ray	toothache

Pass out a different sheet to each of the students in the pair. The students are to complete their sheets by getting the information on their partners' sheets. The partners must not show each other their sheets. Prompt the students to ask questions such as these: When you have a sling, what's wrong? *(You have a broken arm.)* What does the dentist do when you have a toothache? *(He/she makes an X ray of the tooth.)*

4. Role Play

Have students role-play going to a doctor's office. The patient should tell what is wrong, and the doctor should do something, such as take an X ray or give pills. Students could use the list of problems and remedies from activity 3 to help them in this activity. Also, the Focus on Language activity, in which students practice describing ailments, would be helpful background for performing this activity. Again, you might want to act out the situation first to provide a model for students to follow.

WRITING

Have students do these activities independently or as whole-class or group activities.

1. *(Have students draw their own pictures of a person or provide pictures from magazines.)* Label the parts of the body on the picture of the person you have.

2. List things you have used when you were sick.
3. Tell about the pictures in the unit. Write as many sentences as you can to explain what is in the pictures.
4. Describe a time you went to the doctor's or dentist's office. Tell how you felt. Tell what happened.

FOCUS ON LANGUAGE

Present/review the language for talking about physical problems, the equivalent of: My (tooth, ear, arm, etc.) hurts. I have a headache/stomachache/earache. I'm sick. I have a cold.

To review the material, you can point to a part of the body and act out having a problem, and have students describe what's wrong with you.

VOCABULARY

The Doctor's Office	Chez le médecin	La oficina del médico	Beim Arzt	Dal medico
doctor	le médecin	la médica	die Ärztin	la dottoressa
nurse	l'infirmier	el enfermero	die Krankenschwester	l'infermiere
patient	le malade	el paciente	der Patient	il paziente
medicine	les médicaments	la medicina	die Medizin	la medicina
pill	le comprimé	la pastilla	die Pille	la pillola
thermometer	le thermomètre	el termómetro	das Thermometer	il termometro
bandage	le pansement	la venda adhesiva	das Pflaster	il cerotto medicato
cast	le plâtre	la escayola	der Gipsverband	il gesso
sling	l'écharpe	el cabestillo	die Schlinge	il bendaggio a fionda
hypodermic needle	la seringue	la aguja hipodérmica	die Spritze	l'ago
blood	le sang	la sangre	das Blut	il sangue
cane	la canne	el bastón	der Stock	il bastone
crutch	la béquille	la muleta	die Krücke	la gruccia
stethoscope	le stéthoscope	el estetoscopio	das Stethoskop	lo stetoscopio
examining table	la table d'examination	la camilla	der Untersuchungstisch	la tavola da esaminare
sneeze	l'éternuement	el estornudo	das Niesen	lo starnuto
arm	le bras	el brazo	der Arm	il braccio
elbow	le coude	el codo	der Ellbogen	il gomito
hand	la main	la mano	die Hand	la mano
finger	le doigt	el dedo	der Finger	il dito
thumb	le pouce	el pulgar	der Daumen	il pollice
leg	la jambe	la pierna	das Bein	la gamba
wheelchair	le fauteuil roulant	la silla de ruedas	der Rollstuhl	la sedia a rotelle
foot	le pied	el pie	der Fuß	il piede
ankle	la cheville	el tobillo	der Enkel	la caviglia
toe	le doigt de pied	el dedo (del pie)	der Zeh	il dito del piede
shoulder	l'épaule	el hombro	die Schulter	la spalla
back	le dos	la espalda	der Rücken	la schiena
chest	la poitrine	el pecho	die Brust	il petto
knee	le genou	la rodilla	das Knie	il ginocchio

The Dentist's Office	Chez le dentiste	La oficina del dentista	Beim Zahnarzt	Dal dentista
dentist	le dentiste	el dentista	der Zahnarzt	il dentista
dental hygienist	l'assistante	la higienista dental	die Zahnassistentin	l'assistente del dentista
tooth	la dent	el diente	der Zahn	il dente
toothbrush	la brosse à dents	el cepillo de dientes	die Zahnbürste	lo spazzolino da denti
toothpaste	le dentifrice	la pasta dentífrica	die Zahnpaste	il dentifricio
dental floss	le fil dentaire	la seda dental	der Zahnfaden	la bavella
waiting room	la salle d'attente	la sala de espera	das Wartezimmer	l'anticamera
magazines	les revues	las revistas	die Zeitschriften	le riviste
X ray	la radiographie	los rayos X	die Röntgenstrahlen	i raggi X
smile	le sourire	la sonrisa	das Lächeln	il sorriso
lips	les lèvres	los labios	die Lippen	le labbra
tongue	la langue	la lengua	die Zunge	la lingua
eyebrow	le sourcil	la ceja	die Augenbraue	il sopracciglio
eyes	les yeux	los ojos	die Augen	gli occhi
nose	le nez	la nariz	die Nase	il naso
mouth	la bouche	la boca	der Mund	la bocca
chin	le menton	la barbilla	das Kinn	il mento
ear	l'oreille	la oreja	das Ohr	l'orecchio
braces	l'appareil dentaire	los frenos	die Klammern	l'apparecchio per denti
head	la tête	la cabeza	der Kopf	la testa
face	la figure	la cara	das Gesicht	la faccia
cheek	la joue	la mejilla	die Wange	la guancia
forehead	le front	la frente	die Stirn	la fronte

12. The Barber Shop/Beauty Salon

QUESTIONS ABOUT THE PICTURES

1. What do you use to make your hair look neat?
2. Which people cut hair?
3. What can you use to cut your nails?
4. Name some colors of hair. Name the colors of hair of the people in the pictures.
5. Name some hairstyles or ways you can have your hair. Tell about the hairstyles of the people in the picture.
6. *(top picture—bottom center)* What is the woman under the hair dryer doing?
7. *(top picture—top center)* Who is the woman with the scissors? What is she doing?
8. *(bottom picture—center)* Describe the boy in the center in green. What kind of hairstyle does he have? What do you think he has just done?
9. *(bottom picture—center)* Describe the two men looking in the window. What do you think they are going to do?
10. Do you go to a barber/beauty shop to get your hair done?

ACTION STORIES

Possible topics: shampooing your hair, giving a manicure *(nails, nail file),* putting on makeup *(powder, mascara, lipstick)*

Example: Shampooing your hair

1. Your hair is dirty. Shampoo it. 2. Go to the medicine chest. 3. Take out the shampoo. 4. Get a towel. 5. Go to the sink. 6. Wet your hair. 7. Put shampoo on your hair. 8. Wash your hair. Rub hard. 9. Rinse your hair. 10. Get the hair dryer and brush. 11. Dry your hair. 12. Brush it.

GROUP ACTIVITIES

1. Classifying

Have students name as many objects from the picture as they can for each of the following categories: things you use to make your hair neat, people who work in a beauty shop, people who cut hair, hairstyles, colors of hair, things to do with shaving, makeup, things you use on your nails, things you use on or in your hair, things you use to curl your hair.

2. Pantomime

Pantomime actions that use the objects in the pictures. Have students guess the objects you are working with. Examples: using a hair dryer, combing your hair, putting on nail polish, using nail clippers, using a curling iron, putting on makeup, filing your nails.

Extend the activity by using the pantomimes to introduce the verbs that go with the objects. Then have individual students do pantomimes for the class to guess. Encourage the class to answer in complete sentences. Example: She's putting on lipstick. He's cutting his nails with nail clippers.

3. Discussion

Have you ever gone to the barber/beauty shop? What hairstyles are popular with students now/were popular in the past? Lead students in a discussion of these topics.

4. Role Play

Have students role-play being customers in a barber/beauty shop. They need to describe to the hairstylist what they want done to their hair and how they want their hair done: the equivalent of *I'd like my hair cut/washed/blown dry*. You might want to do the activity yourself first to provide a model for students to follow. For beginning classes, you might want to prepare a dialogue for the whole class to practice. For more advanced classes, give roles to the students: for example, a hairstylist who likes short hairstyles and a customer who has always worn his or her hair long.

WRITING

Have students do these activities independently or as whole-class or group activities.

1. Describe your hair.
2. Tell about things you use on your hair to make it look nice.
3. *(Provide pictures from magazines of several people with a variety of hairstyles and colors.)* Describe the person's hair.
4. Tell about the pictures in the unit. Write as many sentences as you can to explain what is in the pictures.
5. Describe a time you went to the barber/beauty shop. Tell what happened.

FOCUS ON LANGUAGE

The vocabulary in the unit focuses on how to describe people's hair. Help students learn the language to describe people more completely by telling about their height and age. Introduce this vocabulary:

height: tall, short, medium height

age: child (boy, girl), teenager, young, middle-aged, senior citizen; about 20, 30, 40, 50, 60

Have students practice the vocabulary by describing people in pictures, as they did in Writing activity 3.

VOCABULARY

The Barber Shop/Beauty Salon	Chez le coiffeur	La peluquería de caballeros y señoras	Beim Herrenfriseur/beim Damenfriseur	Dal barbiere/Istituto di bellezza
hairstylist	le coiffeuse	la peluquera	die Friseuse	la purrucchiera
shampoo	le shampooing	el champú	das Shampoo	lo shampoo
suds	la mousse de savon	la espuma	der Schaum	la schiuma di sapone
comb	le peigne	el peine	der Kamm	il pettine
brush	la brosse	el cepillo	die Bürste	la spazzola
scissors	les ciseaux	las tijeras	die Schere	le forbici
curlers	les rouleaux	los rollos	die Lockenwickel	i bigodini
curling iron	le fer à friser	el rizador	die Lockenschere	il ferro per arricciare i capelli
barber	le coiffeur	el barbero	der Herrenfriseur	il barbiere
shaving cream	la crème à raser	la crema de afeitar	die Rasiercreme	la crema da barba
razor	le rasoir	la navaja de afeitar	das Rasiermesser	il rasoio
beard	la barbe	la barba	der Bart	la barba
mousse	la mousse	la espuma de pelo	der Schaum	il mousse
manicurist	la manucure	la manicura	die Handpflegerin	la manicure
fingernail	l'ongle	la uña	der Fingernagel	l'unghia
nail polish	le vernis à ongles	el esmalte	der Nagellack	lo smalto
lipstick	le rouge à lèvres	el lápiz de labios	der Lippenstift	il rossetto
mascara	le mascara	el rimel	das Maskara	la mascara
powder	la poudre	el polvo	der Puder	la cipra
hair dryer	le sèche-cheveux	el secador	die Trockenhaube	l'asciugacapelli
bald	chauve	calvo	kahl	calvo
mustache	la moustache	el bigote	der Schnurrbart	i baffi
freckles	les taches de rousseur	las pecas	die Sommersprossen	le lentiggini
pedicurist	la pédicure	la pedicura	die Fußpflegerin	la pedicure
barrette	la barrette	el pasador	die Haarspange	il fermacapelli
braid	la tresse	la trenza	der Zopf	la treccia
wavy	ondulé	ondulado	wellig	ondulati
straight	lisse	liso	gerade	stretti
curly	bouclé	rizado	lockig	ricci
short (hair)	court	corto	kurz	corti

long (hair)	long	largo	lang	lunghi
black (hair)	noir	negro	schwarz	neri
brown (hair)	brun	moreno	braun	castagni
blond (hair)	blond	rubio	blond	biondi
red (hair)	roux	pelirrojo	rot	rossi
toenail	l'ongle d'orteil	la uña (del pie)	der Fußnagel	l'unghia del piede
nail clippers	le coupe-ongles	el cortaúñas	die Nagelschere	il tagliaunghie
nail file	la lime à ongles	la lima	die Nagelfeile	la limaiola
crew cut	les cheveux en brosse	el corte a cepillo	der amerikanische Haarschnitt	il taglio a spazzola
ponytail	la queue de cheval	la cola de caballo	der Pferdeschwanz	la coda di cavallo
bangs	la frange	el flequillo	der Pony	la frangia
bun	le chignon	el moño	der Knoten	il chignon
part (in hair)	la raie	la raya	der Scheitel	la scriminatura
hair spray	la laque	la laca	der Haarfestiger	lo spruzzo
hair	les cheveux	el pelo	die Haare	i capelli
blow dryer	le sèche-cheveux	el secador	der Fön	il fon

13. The Post Office/The Bank

QUESTIONS ABOUT THE PICTURES

1. Name three things you send in the mail.
2. Name things you use to wrap a package.
3. *(top left picture)* What is the boy at the counter doing?
4. *(top left picture)* Why are the people waiting in line?
5. *(bottom center picture)* What is the mail carrier doing?
6. Name places in the bank where you can get money.
7. Name three ways you can pay for things.
8. *(bottom right picture)* What is the man with the glasses doing?
9. *(top center picture)* What is boy with the box doing?
10. Why do people use a post-office box/safety deposit box/checkbook/scale in a post office?

ACTION STORIES

Possible topics: how to make a phone call from a phone booth, wrapping a package, mailing and addressing a letter

Example: How to wrap a package

1. You're going to wrap a package to mail. 2. Get the box you want to mail. 3. Wrap paper around the box. 4. Fold the ends down. 5. Put packing tape on the ends. 6. Wrap string around the package. 7. Cut the string with scissors. 8. Make a knot in the string. 9. Stick a label on your package. 10. Write the address of the person receiving the package. 11. Your address is the return address! 12. Your package is ready to go to the post office.

GROUP ACTIVITIES

1. Classifying

Have students name as many objects from the picture as they can for each of the following categories:

post office: things on a letter, places to mail a letter, things you use to wrap a package

bank: people who work in a bank, things you put in your wallet, things to do with checks, things a secretary uses, places where you can get money, things you can use to pay for things you want to buy

2. Pantomime

Pantomime actions that use the objects in the pictures. Have students guess the objects you are working with. Examples: using a phone booth, mailing a letter, putting a stamp on a letter, getting money at the automatic teller, writing a check, typing on a typewriter.

Extend the activity by using the pantomimes to introduce the verbs that go with the objects. Then have individual students do pantomimes for the class to guess. Encourage the class to answer in complete sentences. Example: She's making a phone call in a phone booth. She's taking money out of her wallet.

3. Discussion

Discuss the items in the pictures so that students understand their uses; for example, the scale in a post office, a safety deposit box, a checkbook, a safe, a security camera.

4. Debate

Your class/group has been asked to prepare a package to send to a school in another country. The package is to contain things that show what your school is like. Decide what to include in the package.

5. Discussion

Discuss with students the reasons people use a post office and a bank. Have them tell about times that they have been to the two places.

WRITING

Have students do these activities independently or as whole-class or group activities.

1. *(Supply actual postcards or a sheet on which a postcard is outlined.)* Write a postcard to someone in the country whose language you are studying. Tell about what things you are doing. Be sure to include the address of the person to whom you are writing.
2. *(Supply envelopes.)* Address an envelope to someone in the country whose language you are studying. Be sure to include your address and the postal code.

3. Write a list of things in a wallet.
4. Write about the pictures in the unit. Write as many sentences as you can to explain what is in them.

FOCUS ON LANGUAGE

Present/review the denominations of money in the target language. Present a list of coins and bills in order from those least in value to those highest in value. If possible, show students examples of the money and discuss with them what is pictured on it. Give examples of what you can buy with each of the bills (e.g., you can make a telephone call with a quarter). As an activity, list the cost of several items in the currency and have students practice saying the prices and using the currency names.

VOCABULARY

The Post Office	La poste	El correo	Das Postamt	L'officio postale
letter	la lettre	la carta	der Brief	la lettera
phone booth	la cabine téléphonique	la cabina telefónica	die Telefonzelle	la cabina telefonica
mailbox	la boîte aux lettres	el buzón	der Briefkasten	la cassetta postale
mail slot	la fente	la ranura	der Briefeinwurf	il buco delle lettere
postal worker	l'employé des postes	el empleado postal	der Postbeamte (m.)	l'impiegato dell'ufficio postale
postcard	la carte postale	la tarjeta postal	die Postkarte	la cartolina
return address	l'expéditeur	el remitente	der Absender	l'indirizzo del mittente
address	l'adresse	la dirección	die Adresse	l'indirizzo
zip code	le code postal	el código postal	die Postleitzahl	il codice postale
mailbag	le sac postal	la bolsa de correo	der Briefsack	il sacco da posta
stamp	le timbre	el sello	die Briefmarke	il francobollo
string	la ficelle	el cordel	die Schnur	lo spago
knot	le nœud	el nudo	der Knoten	il nodo
packing tape	le ruban adhésif	la cinta	der Klebstreifen	il nastro d'imballaggio
scale	la balance	la balanza	die Waage	la bilancia
post-office box	la boîte postale	el apartado postal	das Postfach	la cassetta per imbucare
label	l'étiquette	la etiqueta	das Etikett	l'etichetta
bow	le nœud	el lazo	die Schleife	il fiocco
package	le paquet	el paquete	das Paket	il pacco
ink pad	le tampon encreur	el tampón de entintar	das Stempelkissen	il tampone
rubber stamp	le tampon	el sello de goma	der Stempel	il timbro
rubber band	l'élastique	la cinta de goma	das Gummiband	l'elastico
postmark	le cachet de la poste	el matasellos	der Poststempel	il timbro postale

The Bank	La banque	El banco	Die Bank	La banca
teller	la caissière	la cajera	die Kassiererin	il cassiere
bill	le billet	el billete	der Schein	il conto
check	le chèque	el cheque	der Scheck	l'assegno
piggy bank	la tirelire	la hucha	das Sparschwein	il salvadanaio
drive-in	le drive-in	el servicio para automovilistas	die Einfahrbank	il servizio per le automobili

wallet	le portefeuille	la billetera	der Geldbeutel	il portafoglio
coin	la pièce de monnaie	la moneda	die Münze	la moneta
checkbook	le chéquier	el talonario de cheques	das Scheckbuch	il libretto d'assegni
signature	la signature	la firma	die Unterschrift	la firma
automatic teller	le guichet automatique	el cajero automático	der automatische Geldabheber	il bancomat
key	la clé	la llave	der Schlüssel	la chiave
lock	la serrure	la cerradura	das Schloß	la serratura
paper clip	le trombone	el sujetapapeles	die Büroklammer	la graffa
security camera	la caméra de surveillance	la cámara de seguridad	die Sicherheitskamera	la telecamera di sicurezza
credit card	la carte de crédit	la tarjeta de crédito	die Kreditkarte	la tessera di credito
safety deposit box	le coffre	la caja de seguridad	das Sicherheitsfach	la cassetta di sicurezza
file cabinet	le classeur	el archivo	der Aktenschrank	lo schedario
security guard	le gardien	el guardia de seguridad	die Wache	la guardia
safe	le coffre-fort	la caja fuerte	der Tresor	la cassaforte
typewriter	la machine à écrire	la máquina de escribir	die Schreibmaschine	la macchina da scrivere
notepad	le bloc-notes	el cuaderno	der Notizblock	il blocco
receptionist	la réceptioniste	la recepcionista	die Empfangsdame	la segretaria

14. At the Gas Station

QUESTIONS ABOUT THE PICTURE

1. Where do you go to get gas in the gas station?
2. What vehicle pulls cars when they break down?
3. What vehicles do you see in the picture?
4. *(bottom left)* In what part of the car is the dog/doll?
5. What do you see in the upper left corner of the picture?
6. *(lower right)* What is the boy doing with his bicycle?
7. *(center)* Describe the mechanic next to the race car. What is he wearing? What is he doing?
8. What is/are a jack/windshield wipers/headlights used for?
9. What are things you can buy/do at a gas station?
10. Have you ever ridden a bicycle or a tricycle?

ACTION STORIES

Possible topics: how to ride a bicycle, how to get into a car *(door handle, passenger's seat, seat belt, steering wheel)*

Example: How to ride a bicycle

1. Let's go for a bike ride. 2. Kick up the kickstand. 3. Put your hand on the handlebar. 4. Put one leg over the seat and sit on the bike. 5. Put both hands on the handlebars. 6. Put your feet on the pedals. 7. Pedal the bike. 8. Oops! You're going too fast. 9. Use the hand brake. 10. Stop the bike.

GROUP ACTIVITIES

1. Classifying

Have students name as many objects from the picture as they can for each of the following categories: vehicles, parts of a bicycle, parts of a car that are inside, parts of a car that are outside, tools in a gas station, things that have to do with a tire.

2. Chanting

With students, prepare sentences describing the parts of the car and their uses. Have students chant the sentences. Examples: An engine makes the car run. A hood is in the front of the car; it covers the engine. Headlights light the road in front of the car at night. The trunk holds things to take with you on a trip. Example chant: An engine, engine, engine makes the car, car run.

3. Guessing Game

Have students play a game like Twenty Questions, using parts of the car. Give a student a card with the name of a part of the car. The rest of the class has to guess the part, posing questions such as: Is it outside the car? Can you sit on it? Can you put things in it? Does it turn?

4. Memory Game

Have students work in pairs or small groups. They are not to look at the picture. Have them write down the names of (or draw) as many things as they can remember from the picture. Have groups compare their answers.

WRITING

Have students do these activities independently or as whole-class or group activities.

1. *(Have students draw their own pictures of a car or provide pictures from magazines.)* Label the parts of the car.
2. *(Have students draw their own pictures of a bicycle or provide pictures from magazines.)* Label the parts of the bicycle.
3. Write about a special car or bicycle trip you have taken.
4. Imagine someone wants to take a bicycle ride through your town or city. Write down what the person should see and do.
5. You are given a magic bike. What does it do that is special? Does it float? Does it go very fast? Tell about your ride on it.

FOCUS ON LANGUAGE

Have students describe the parts of the car, using prepositions and phrases of location: *inside, outside, in the front of the car, in the back of the car, under the car.* Have students point to a part of the car and describe its location in a sentence.

VOCABULARY

At the Gas Station	À la station-service	En la gasolinera	Auf der Tankstelle	Alla stazione di servizio
mechanic	le mécanicien	el mecánico	der Mechaniker	il meccanico
oil	l'huile	el aceite	das Öl	l'olio
rag	le chiffon	el trapo	der Lumpen	il cencio
tow truck	la dépanneuse	la grúa	der Abschlepper	il carro attrezzi
truck driver	le camionneur	el camionero	der Lastwagenfahrer	il camionista
tank truck	le camion-citerne	el camión tanque	der Tanker	l'autocisterna
bicycle	le vélo	la bicicleta	das Fahrrad	la bicicletta
hand brake	le frein à main	el freno manual	die Handbremse	il freno a mano
bicycle chain	la chaîne de vélo	la cadena de bicicleta	die Fahrradkette	la catena
spokes	les rayons	los rayos	die Speichen	i raggi
training wheels	les roulettes	las ruedas de entrenamiento	die Übungsräder	le ruote speciali
coveralls	les bleus de travail	el mono	der Overall	la tuta
race car	la voiture de course	el coche de carreras	das Rennauto	la macchina da corsa
sunroof	le toit ouvrant	el techo de sol	das Schiebedach	il tettino
garage	le garage	el garaje	die Garage	il garage
car wash	le lave-auto	el lavado de coches	die Autoreinigung	l'autolavaggio
gas cap	le bouchon de réservoir d'essence	el casco del tanque de gasolina	der Tankverschluß	il coperchio del serbatoio
tricycle	le tricycle	el triciclo	das Dreirad	il triciclo
handlebars	le guidon de vélo	el manillar	die Lenkstange	il manubrio di bicicletta
reflectors	les réflecteurs	los reflectores	die Rückstrahler	i riflettori
pedal	la pédale	el pedal	das Pedal	il pedale
kickstand	la béquille	el soporte	der Fahrradstand	il cavalletto
jack	le cric	el gato	der Wagenheber	il cricco
gas pump	la pompe à essence	el surtidor de gasolina	die Benzinpumpe	la pompa della benzina
pliers	les pinces	los alicates	die Zange	la pinza
dashboard	le tableau de bord	el tablero de instrumentos	das Armaturenbrett	il cruscotto
backseat	le siège arrière	el asiento posterior	der Rücksitz	il sedile posteriore
driver's seat	la place du conducteur	el asiento del conductor	der Fahrersitz	il sedile del guidatore
passenger's seat	le siège de passager	el asiento del pasajero	der Beifahrersitz	il sedile del passeggero
seat belt	la ceinture de sécurité	el cinturón de seguridad	der Sitzgurt	la cintura di sicurezza

hood	le capot	el capó	die Schutzhaube	il cofano
engine	le moteur	el motor	der Motor	il motore
trunk	le coffre	el baúl	der Kofferraum	il portabagagli
fender	l'aile	el guardalodo	der Kotflügel	il paraurti
flat tire	le pneu à plat	la llanta reventada	die Panne	la gomma a terra
tire	le pneu	la llanta	der Reifen	la gomma
hubcap	l'enjoliveur	el tapacubos	die Nabe	il coprimozzo
headlight	le phare	el faro	der Scheinwerfer	il fanalo
brake lights	les feux arrière	los faros de freno	die Bremslichter	le luci dei freni
windshield	le pare-brise	el parabrisas	die Windschutzscheibe	il parabrezza
windshield wipers	les essuie-glaces	los limpiaparabrisas	die Scheibenwischer	il tergicristallo
steering wheel	le volant	el volante	das Lenkrad	il volante
rearview mirror	le rétroviseur	el espejo retrovisor	der Rückspiegel	lo specchietto retrovisore
air hose	la pompe à air	la manga de aire	der Luftschlauch	il manicotto dell'aria
door handle	la poignée de portière	la manilla	der Türgriff	la maniglia

15. People in Our Community

QUESTIONS ABOUT THE PICTURE

1. Who works on the radio and introduces songs?
2. Which people work with flowers and plants?
3. What does a carpenter do? (makes things from wood; builds
4. What does a tailor do?
5. What is the astronomer doing in the picture? What do astronomers do?
6. What is the salesman doing?
7. Which people wear a special uniform for their job?
8. Which people in your community do you know?
9. What jobs do people you know do?
10. Discuss what each of the people in the picture does. Why is his or her job important?

ACTION STORIES

Possible topics: jobs and typical actions, delivering mail (being a letter carrier), driving a bus (being a school bus driver)

Example: Jobs and typical actions

1. A secretary types letters. Type a letter. 2. A painter paints walls. Take a brush and paint the wall. 3. A librarian helps people check out books. Stamp a book. 4. A school bus driver drives a bus. Drive a bus. 5. A cowboy lassoes animals. Lasso a calf. 6. A fire fighter puts out fires. Pick up a hose and put water on the fire. 7. A carpenter cuts wood. Pick up a saw and cut wood. 8. A doorman takes care of baggage. Pick up a suitcase. 9. A photographer takes pictures. Take a picture. 10. A police officer directs traffic. Direct traffic.

GROUP ACTIVITIES

1. Classifying

Have students name as many people from the picture as they can for each of the following categories: sells things, works with books, usually works outside, usually works inside, repairs things, draws things, helps people/animals who are sick.

2. Chanting

Prepare two-part chants for students to perform. The first part names a profession; the second part describes a typical activity of the job.

Examples:

He's a plumber.	He fixes sinks.
He's a tailor.	He fixes clothes.
She's a florist.	She sells flowers.
He's reporter.	He writes stories for the newspaper.

At first, prompt students with the first part and have them chant the second. Later point to the job in the picture and have students chant both parts.

3. Pantomime

Have students pantomime doing different jobs and have the class guess the job each student is pantomiming (e.g., putting letters into a mailbox, modeling clothes, etc.). Extend the activity by using the pantomimes to introduce the verbs that describe the activities being pantomimed. Encourage the class to answer in complete sentences. Example: She's a pharmacist. She's putting pills into a bottle.

4. Guessing Game

Have students play a game resembling Twenty Questions. Give a student a card with the name of a job. The rest of the class has to guess the job, posing questions such as: Do you work outside? Do you work with people? Do you wear a uniform? Do you fix things?

5. Interview

Have students role-play being a person who has one of the jobs in the picture. The rest of the class asks questions about the job such as: What is a typical day in your job? What do you like about your job? What don't you like about your job? Do you make a lot of money? What do you need to know to do your job? For lower-level classes, take the role of the person in the occupation and simply have students ask the questions.

WRITING

Have students do these activities independently or as whole-class or group activities.

1. List people in your community whom you know and who help you.
2. Draw a picture with people doing different jobs. Label each picture.

3. What job would you like to do best? Tell why.
4. Choose a job. Make up a story about what happens to a person doing the job on an unusual day.

FOCUS ON LANGUAGE

With the students, prepare lists of words associated with each job.

Example: mail carrier (packages, letters, mailbox, doorbell, deliver)

Have students draw a picture with a person doing the job, and have them illustrate several words in the word association. Several of the jobs relate to vocabulary in other units: cook (unit 10, In a Restaurant), artist (unit 1, Our Classroom).

VOCABULARY

People in Our Community	Les gens de notre quartier	Las personas de nuestra comunidad	Leute in unserer Umgebung	La gente nella communità
saleswoman	la vendeuse	la vendedora	die Verkäuferin	la commessa
electrician	l'électricien	el electricista	der Elektriker	l'elettricista
judge	la juge	la juez	die Richterin	il giudice
cook	le cuisinier	el cocinero	der Koch	il cuoco
model	le mannequin	la modelo	das Mannequin	l'indossatrice
construction worker	le constructeur	el obrero	der Bauarbeiter	il manovale
policewoman	la femme-agent	la policía	die Polizistin	la donna poliziotto
veterinarian	la vétérinaire	la veterinaria	die Tierärztin	il veterinario
disc jockey	le disc-jockey	el disc jockey	der Discjockey	il disc jockey
reporter	le journaliste	el periodista	der Reporter	il cronista
architect	l'architecte	la arquitecta	die Architektin	l'architetto
athlete	l'athlète	el atleta	der Sportler	l'atleta
doorman	le portier	el portero	der Portier	il portiere
fire fighter	le pompier	el bombero	die Feuerwehrfrau	il pompiere
florist	la fleuriste	la florera	die Blumenhändlerin	la fiorista
tailor	le tailleur	el sastre	der Schneider	il sarto
factory worker	l'ouvrière	la trabajadora de fábrica	die Fabrikarbeiterin	l'operaia
bus driver	la conductrice d'autobus	la conductora de autobús	der Busfahrer	il guidatore dell'autobus
television repairer	le réparateur de télévision	el reparador de televisión	der Fernsehmechaniker	il tecnico video
taxi driver	le chauffeur de taxi	el taxista	der Taxifahrer	il tassista
plumber	le plombier	el plomero	der Installateur	l'idraulico
optician	l'opticienne	la oculista	die Optikerin	l'ottico
butcher	le boucher	el carnicero	der Metzger	il macellaio
jeweler	le bijoutier	el joyero	der Juwelier	il gioielliere
foreman	le chef d'équipe	el capataz	der Bauleiter	il capomastro
fashion designer	la couturière	la diseñadora de modas	die Modeschöpferin	la stilista
tour guide	l'organisatrice de voyages	la guía	der Tourleiter	la guida
bookseller	le libraire	el librero	der Buchhändler	il venditore di libri
librarian	le bibliothécaire	el bibliotecario	der Bibliothekar	il bibliotecario
artist	l'artiste	la artista	die Künstlerin	l'artista

pharmacist	la pharmacienne	la farmacéutica	die Apothekerin	la farmacista
carpenter	le charpentier	el carpintero	der Schreiner	il falegname
sailor	le marin	el marinero	der Schiffer	il marinaio
banker	le banquier	la banquera	die Bankbeamtin	il banchiere
lawyer	l'avocate	la abogada	die Rechtsanwältin	l'avvocatessa
computer programmer	la programmeuse	la programadora de computadoras	die Komputerprogrammiererin	il programmatore
photographer	le photographe	el fotógrafo	der Fotograf	il fotografo
gardener	le jardinier	el jardinero	der Gärtner	il giardiniere
paramedic	l'auxiliaire médical	el auxiliar del médico	die Artzthelferin	l'assistente del medico
letter carrier	le facteur	el cartero	der Briefträger	il postino
secretary	la secrétaire	la secretaria	die Sekretärin	la segretaria
painter	le peintre	el pintor	der Anstreicher	il pittore
weather forecaster	le météorologue	el meteorólogo	der Wetteransager	il meteorologo
salesman	le vendeur	el vendedor	der Verkäufer	il commesso
cowboy	le cow-boy	el vaquero	der Cowboy	il cowboy
astronomer	l'astronome	el astrónomo	der Astronom	l'astronomo
policeman	l'agent de police	el policía	der Polizist	il poliziotto
fisherman	le pêcheur	el pescador	der Fischer	il pescatore

16. Going Places (Transportation)

QUESTIONS ABOUT THE PICTURE

1. Name three things that move in the air/water.
2. What kinds of transportation do you see on a city street?
3. What are the three biggest vehicles in the picture?
4. What do the colors of traffic lights mean?
5. *(center of picture)* What things are the children on the sidewalk using to play?
6. *(lower left)* What is the boy doing? Is he working hard?
7. You are a pedestrian, a person who walks. What things on a city street do you use?
8. How do you get to school?
9. What means of transportation have you taken on trips?
10. What are the advantages of taking an airplane/a train?

ACTION STORIES

Possible topics: crossing the street, going to wait for a bus *(street, intersection, bus stop, crosswalk),* how to roller skate, a boat ride

Example: Crossing the street

1. Walk to the intersection. 2. Look at the traffic lights. 3. The light is yellow. Wait! 4. Now the light is red for "Stop!" Wait a few seconds. 5. Now the light is green. 6. Look both ways for cars coming. Go! 7. Walk in the crosswalk. 8. Cross the street. 9. Step up on the sidewalk. 10. We've crossed the street!

GROUP ACTIVITIES

1. Classifying

a. Put the following chart on the board or on a transparency. Have students complete the chart by indicating the information appropriate for each vehicle. Then have students describe each vehicle. For example: A car goes on the ground/street. It has four wheels and a motor, and it is made of metal.

	goes on ground/ air/water	has wheels	number of wheels	has motor	made of metal
car					
scooter					
truck					
camper					
stroller					
airplane					
canoe					
ship					

b. Have students name as many objects from the picture as they can for each of the following categories: things you see on a city street, things you see near the ocean, things that a motor moves, things that people move themselves, vehicles in which people can sleep overnight, things that help protect people, dangerous vehicles.

2. Discussion

Lead students in a discussion of the differences between the various groups of vehicles: boat (canoe, rowboat, cruise ship, sailboat, tugboat); car (car, jeep, taxi), truck (truck, van, fire engine, ambulance, cement mixer). The discussion should focus on the size and propulsion of the vehicle (A cruise ship is bigger than a boat; the wind moves a sailboat) or on the use of the vehicle (Fire fighters use a fire engine to go to a fire. A fire engine has ladders for fire fighters). Have students produce sentences, orally or in writing, that explain the differences among the vehicles.

3. Debate

Present the following questions to the group: You can choose to ride in any two vehicles in which you have never ridden. Which two do you choose? Why did you choose them? *(it is fun, it goes fast, you see many things from the air, etc.)* Have each student write down his or her choices. Have students compare their answers and defend their choices. At the end of the discussion, take a vote to see which vehicles are the ones that most students want to try out.

4. Be Inventors

Present the following activity to the class:

> Invent a new vehicle. It might have parts of other vehicles that you know. For example, it could be a car-helicopter with a propeller on the top or a canoe with a hot-air balloon on the top or roller skates with a motor. Draw a picture of your vehicle and describe its parts. Explain why it will be useful.

WRITING

Have students do these activities independently or as whole-class or group activities.

1. List all the kinds of transportation you have used.
2. List all the kinds of transportation in the picture that you have not used.
3. Have you ever taken a trip to another city/town? Write about how you got there. Was the trip fun or boring? What did you see on the way? Where did you eat?
4. You can get from home to school or to some other place in your town in an unusual way. Describe your trip. Try to use at least four vehicles in your trip. For example, you might take a canoe across the river near your house, or you might take a balloon for part of the trip.

FOCUS ON LANGUAGE

Present/review verbs that go with vehicles. For example, present the equivalent of these expressions: get on/get off, ride (a bus)/ride in a train, drive (a car, truck), pay the bus fare. Have students draw pictures to illustrate the verbs, using the vehicles in the unit.

VOCABULARY

Going Places	En voyage	El transporte	Unterwegs	Transporto
car	la voiture	el coche	das Auto	la macchina
hang glider	le deltaplane	el planeador	das Segelflugzeug	l'aliante
sail	la voile	la vela	das Segel	la vela
sailboat	le bateau à voile	el barco de vela	das Segelboot	la barca a vela
tugboat	le remorqueur	el barco remolcador	der Schlepper	il rimorchiatore
train	le train	el tren	der Zug	il treno
taxi	le taxi	el taxi	das Taxi	il tassì
stroller	la poussette	el cochecito de niño	der Sportwagen	il passeggino
baby carriage	la voiture d'enfant	el cochecito	der Kinderwagen	la carrozzina
cement mixer	la bétonnière	el mezclador de cemento	der Zementmixer	la betoniera
bus	l'autobus	el autobús	der Bus	l'autobus
school bus	l'autobus scolaire	el autobús escolar	der Schulbus	l'autobus per scuola
airplane	l'avion	el avión	das Flugzeug	l'aereo
hot-air balloon	la montgolfière	el globo	der Ballon	il pallone
helicopter	l'hélicoptère	el helicóptero	der Hubschrauber	l'elicottero
rowboat	le canot à rames	el bote de remos	das Ruderboot	la barca a remi
cruise ship	le paquebot	el crucero	der Passagierdampfer	la nave
motorboat	le canot à moteur	la lancha	das Motorboot	il motoscafo
police car	la voiture de police	el coche de policía	das Polizeiauto	la macchina da polizia
truck	le camion	el camión	der Lastwagen	il camion
fire engine	la voiture de pompiers	el coche de bomberos	das Feuerwehrauto	l'autopompa
ambulance	l'ambulance	la ambulancia	der Krankenwagen	il prontosoccorso
motorcycle	la moto	la motocicleta	das Motorrad	la motocicletta
lighthouse	le phare	el faro	der Leuchtturm	il faro
jeep	la jeep	el jeep	der Jeep	il jeep
van	la camionnette	la camioneta	der Kombiwagen	il furgone
scooter	la trottinette	el patinete	der Roller	il monopattino
skateboard	la planche à roulettes	la tabla de patines	das Skateboard	lo skateboard
roller skates	les patins à roulettes	los patines de ruedas	die Rollschuhe	i pattini a rotelle
canoe	le canoë	la canoa	das Kanu	la canoa
blimp	le dirigeable	el dirigible	das Luftschiff	il dirigibile

camper	la caravane	la caravana	der Wohnwagen	il camper
bicycle	la bicyclette	la bicicleta	das Fahrrad	la bicicletta
traffic lights	les feux de circulation	las luces de tráfico	die Verkehrsampeln	il semaforo
Stop! (red light)	Arrêtez!	¡Alto!	Halt!	stop
Wait! (yellow light)	Attendez!	¡Espere!	Warte!	aspetta
Go! (green light)	Passez!	¡Adelante!	Geh!	avanti
street	la rue	la calle	die Straße	la strada
intersection	le carrefour	la intersección	die Straßenkreuzung	l'incrocio
sidewalk	le trottoir	la acera	der Bürgersteig	il marciapiede
dock	le quai	el muelle	der Pier	il molo
bus stop	l'arrêt d'autobus	la parada de autobús	die Bushaltestelle	la fermata
bridge	le pont	el puente	die Brücke	il ponte
crosswalk	le passage clouté	el cruce de peatones	die Fußgängerkreuzung	il passaggio pedonale
oar	la rame	el remo	das Ruder	il remo
boat	le bateau	el barco	das Boot	la barca
stop sign	le stop	la señal de alto	das Haltesignal	lo stop

17. The Airport

QUESTIONS ABOUT THE PICTURE

1. Who flies an airplane?
2. Where do airplanes land?
3. Name three parts of an airplane.
4. Name four things people might carry on planes.
5. What does a flight attendant/air-traffic controller do?
6. What part of the airport do you see in each of the round pictures?
7. What is happening in the check-in area?
8. What is happening in the customs area? What do people usually do in the customs area?
9. What does a passenger do before getting on an airplane?
10. Have you ever taken a plane? What did you do in the airport?

ACTION STORIES

Possible topics: checking in at the airport, getting on an airplane, packing a suitcase

Example: Checking in at the airport

1. Go to the check-in counter. 2. Wait in line. 3. Now it's your turn. 4. Put your suitcase on the scale. 5. Show your ticket to the ticket agent. 6. Get your boarding pass. 7. Go through the metal detector. Beep! Beep! 8. Take the keys out of your pocket.

GROUP ACTIVITIES

1. Classifying

Have students name as many things from the picture as they can for each of the following categories: people who work in the airport, people who work on an airplane, places in the airport, parts of an airplane, things in an airplane, things to take on a trip.

2. Ordering

a. Have students make a list of things that they see when they go into an airport to take a trip. Tell them to put the list in the order in which they typically see things. Have students/groups write down and compare their answers.

b. Have students make a list of things that they see when they are getting off an airplane in the order in which they see them. Have students/groups write down and compare their answers.

3. Interview

Have students role-play being a person who has one of the jobs in the picture, such as a pilot and a flight attendant. The rest of the class asks questions about the job such as: What is a typical day in your job? What do you like about your job? What don't you like about your job? Do you make a lot of money? Do you visit many places?

WRITING

Have students do these activities independently or as whole-class or group activities.

1. List things you see as you walk through an airport.
2. Make three columns: in the first column, list things you see in the airport building; in the second column, list things you see outside the airport building; in the third column, list things you see on or in the airplane.
3. Have you ever taken an airplane trip? Write about it.
4. Have you ever taken a class trip? Write about it.

FOCUS ON LANGUAGE

Present/review verbs that deal with airplanes/airports. For example, present the equivalent of these expressions: land, take off, get on, get off, arrive, depart. Have students draw pictures illustrating the verbs.

VOCABULARY

The Airport	**L'aéroport**	**El aeropuerto**	**Der Flughafen**	**L'aeroporto**
pilot	le pilote	el piloto	der Pilot	il pilota
copilot	la copilote	la copiloto	der Kopilot	la seconda pilota
navigator	le navigateur	el navegante	der Navigationsoffizier	il navigatore
flight attendant	le steward	el auxiliar de vuelo	der Steward	l'assistente di volo
baggage handler	le bagagiste	el mozo de equipaje	die Gepäckträger	il portabaglio
porter	le porteur	el mozo	der Gepäckträger	il facchino
baggage claim	le service des bagages	la contraseña de equipaje	die Gepäckabnahme	il ritiro bagagli
baggage check-in	l'enregistrement de bagages	el registro de equipaje	die Gepäckannahme	lo sportello bagagli
ticket counter	le guichet	el mostrador de boletos	der Schalter	lo sportello dei biglietti
ticket agent	l'agent de billets	el vendedor de boletos	der Beamte	il bigliettaio
ticket	le billet	el boleto	die Flugkarte	il biglietto
air-traffic controller	la contrôleuse de navigation aérienne	la controladora de tráfico	der Luftverkehrskontrolleur	il controllore di volo
headset	le casque à écouteurs	el juego de auriculares	der Kopfhörer	la cuffia
control tower	la tour de contrôle	la torre de control	der Kontrollturm	la torre di controllo
radar screen	l'écran de radar	la pantalla de radar	der Radarschirm	lo schermo di radar
flags	les drapeaux	las banderas	die Fahnen	le bandiere
elevator	l'ascenseur	el ascensor	der Aufzug	l'ascensore
metal detector	le détecteur de métal	el indicador de metales	der Metalldetektor	il revelatore del metallo
escalator	l'escalier roulant	la escalera mecánica	die Rolltreppe	la scala mobile
gate	la porte	la puerta	die Schranke	la porta
baggage cart	le chariot à bagages	el carrito de equipaje	der Gepäckkarren	il carrello per bagagli
customs officer	la douanière	la aduanera	die Zollbeamtin	l'agente doganale
airplane	l'avion	el avión	das Flugzeug	l'aereo
propeller	l'hélice	la hélice	der Propeller	l'elica
wing	l'aile	el ala	der Flügel	l'ala
engine	le moteur	el motor	der Motor	il motore
landing gear	l'atterrisseur	el tren de aterrizaje	das Fahrgestell	il carrello d'atterraggio
runway	la piste	la pista	die Laufbahn	la pista
hangar	le hangar	el hangar	die Flugzeughalle	l'aviorimessa
Concorde	le Concorde	el Concorde	die Concorde	il Concorde

luggage compartment	le coffre à bagages	la sección de equipaje	der Gepäckraum	il deposito bagagli
seat	le siège	el asiento	der Sitz	il sedile
passenger	le passager	el pasajero	der Passagier	il passeggero
snack bar	le snack-bar	la cafetería	die Imbißstube	la tavola calda
passport	le passeport	el pasaporte	der Paß	il passaporto
video camera	la caméra	la cámara de video	die Bildkamera	il video camera
tennis racket	la raquette de tennis	la raqueta de tenis	der Tennisschläger	la racchetta
binoculars	les jumelles	los prismáticos	der Feldstecher	il binocolo
camera	l'appareil-photo	la cámara	die Kamera	la macchina fotografica
purse	le sac à main	el bolso	die Handtasche	la borsa
suitcase	la valise	la maleta	der Koffer	la valigia
garment bag	le sac à vêtements	la maleta para vestidos y trajes	die Kleiderhülle	il sacco per abiti
briefcase	la serviette	la cartera	die Aktentasche	la borsa per documenti

18. Sports

QUESTIONS ABOUT THE PICTURES

1. What is the name of the sport for which you need a bicycle?
2. What sports take place in or on water?
3. For which sports do you need an animal?
4. For which sports do you need a net or a basket?
5. What might you get when you win at a sport?
6. Which sports require a great deal of running?
7. Which sports are track sports?
8. Which sports can be dangerous?
9. What sports do you play in your school/outside of school?
10. Which sports are popular in the country/countries whose language you are learning?

ACTION STORIES

Possible topics: playing basketball, playing tennis, swimming

Example: Playing basketball

1. Get the ball. 2. Bounce the ball. 3. Run toward the basket. 4. Jump up with the ball. 5. Shoot the ball. 6. Hooray! The ball went through the hoop. I get 2 points.

GROUP ACTIVITIES

1. Classifying

Have students name as many things from the pictures as they can for each of the following categories: sports you can play by yourself, sports that require two or more people, sports that are always played by teams, sports that use a ball, sports that use animals, winter sports, things you need to play football, sports in which you hit a ball.

2. Pantomime

Have students pantomime playing the sports in the pictures. Have the rest of the group guess the sports. Extend the activity by using the pantomimes to introduce the verbs that go with the objects. Encourage the class to answer in complete sentences. Example: She's playing tennis. She's hitting the ball with her racket. She's serving the ball.

3. Word Association

Have students draw a word association picture for a sport they like. Students should choose their sport and make up a list of related words. For example, basketball, *place:* court, basket/hoop, rim, center court; *special clothing:* running shoes, uniform; *actions:* run, jump, throw, pass. You will probably need to supply students with words or, if they are advanced, encourage them to use dictionaries. Have students draw items from their lists and label the items.

4. Group Project: Survey

Have students prepare five questions for a survey about sports. Possible questions include: Which is the best sport to watch? Which is the best sport to play? What is your favorite team? Who is your favorite player/athlete? Have each student ask the questions to three or four students and three or four people outside of class and write down his or her findings. Have students compare their answers.

WRITING

Have students do these activities independently or as whole-class or group activities.

1. List all the sports you have played.
2. List all the sports you have seen on television.
3. Write about your favorite sport or about a time you played your favorite sport.

FOCUS ON LANGUAGE

Present/review the language for talking about sports that they *know how to* play and that they *enjoy*. Have students make up sentences telling what they can do or enjoy doing.

Example: I know how to play baseball/skate. I enjoy skating.

Students can make two illustrations: one showing sports that they enjoy playing, the other showing sports that they know how to play.

VOCABULARY

Sports	Le sport	Los deportes	Der Sport	Sport
gymnastics	la gymnastique	la gimnasia	das Geräteturnen	la ginnastica
goggles	les lunettes de protection	las gafas protectoras	die Schußbrille	gli occhiali di protezione
wrestling	la lutte	la lucha libre	das Ringen	la lotta sportiva
cross-country skiing	le ski de fond	el esquí nórdico	das Schilaufen	il fondo
umpire	l'arbitre	el árbitro	der Schiedsrichter	l'arbitro
bowling	le bowling	jugar a los bolos	das Kegeln	il gioco dei birilli automatici
boxing gloves	les gants de boxe	los guantes de boxeo	die Boxhandschuhe	i guantoni
cycling	le cyclisme	el ciclismo	das Radfahren	il ciclismo
soccer	le football	el fútbol	das Fußballspiel	il calcio
long jump	le saut en longueur	el salto largo	der Weitsprung	il salto in lungo
car racing	la course de voitures	las carreras de coches	das Autorennen	la corsa
baseball	la balle de base-ball	la pelota (de béisbol)	der Baseball	la palla
high jump	le saut en hauteur	el salto alto	der Hochsprung	il salto in alto
table tennis	le tennis de table	el tenis de mesa	das Tischtennisspiel	il ping-pong
skydiving	le parachutisme	el salto libre con paracaídas	das Fallschirmspringen	il paracadutismo
soccer ball	le ballon de football	la pelota (de fútbol)	der Fußball	la palla
boxing	la boxe	el boxeo	das Boxen	il pugilato
badminton	le badminton	el badminton	das Federballspiel	il volano
net	le filet	la red	das Netz	la rete
bat	la batte	el bate	das Schlagholz	la mazza
football	le ballon de football américain	la pelota (de fútbol americano)	der amerikanische Fußball	la palla
parachute	le parachute	el paracaídas	der Fallschirm	il paracadute
swimming pool	la piscine	la piscina	das Schwimmbad	la piscina
running	la course à pied	el correr	das Laufen	il correre
skates	les patins	los patines	die Schlittschuhe	i pattini
skating	le patinage	el patinaje	das Eislaufen	il pattinaggio
hurdles	le saut de haies	las vallas	das Hürdenrennen	la corsa a ostacoli
football	le football américain	el fútbol americano	das amerikanische Fußballspiel	il football americano
golf club	le bâton de golf	el palo de golf	der Golfschläger	la mazza da golf

downhill skiing	le ski	el esquí alpino	der Abfahrtslauf	lo sci alpino
trophy	le trophée	el trofeo	die Trophäe	il trofeo
horse racing	les courses de chevaux	las carreras de caballos	das Pferderennen	la corsa da cavalli
helmet	le casque	el casco	der Helm	l'elmetto
golf	le golf	el golf	das Golfspiel	il golf
medal	la médaille	la medalla	die Medaille	la medaglia
horseback riding	l'équitation	la equitación	das Reiten	l'equitazione
baseball	le base-ball	el béisbol	das Baseballspiel	il baseball
skis	les skis	los esquís	die Schier	gli sci
bicycle	la bicyclette	la bicicleta	das Fahrrad	la bicicletta
volleyball	le volley-ball	el voleibol	das Flugballspiel	la pallavolo
racket	la raquette	la raqueta	der Schläger	la racchetta
jogging	le jogging	el jogging	das Joggen	il footing
hockey	le hockey	el hockey	das Hockey	l' hockey
tennis	le tennis	el tenis	das Tennisspiel	il tennis
diving	la plongeon	el salto al agua	das Tauchen	il tuffarsi
weight lifting	les haltères	el levantamiento de pesos	das Gewichtheben	il sollevamento di pesi
sailing	la voile	la navegación	das Segeln	l'andare a vela
basketball	le basket	el baloncesto	das Korbballspiel	la pallacanestro
swimming	la natation	la natación	das Schwimmen	il nuoto
referee	l'arbitre	el árbitro	der Schiedsrichter	l'arbitro

19. The Talent Show

QUESTIONS ABOUT THE PICTURE

1. Who are the people on the stage?
2. Who are the people at the lower right?
3. Name three places in the picture.
4. Name two instruments in the band.
5. Which instruments do you blow into?
6. What does a master of ceremonies do?
7. *(upper left)* What is the teacher holding? What is she doing?
8. *(lower left)* What is the actress in the dressing room doing?
9. Have you ever played a musical instrument? Which?
10. Have you ever been in a talent show or been on stage? What did you do?

ACTION STORIES

Possible topics: be a one-person orchestra (play the piano, accordion, cymbals, drum, etc.), getting ready to go on stage

Example: Getting ready to go on stage

1. Get ready for the show. 2. Put on some makeup. 3. Put on your costume. 4. Put on your wig. 5. Look in the mirror. You look great! 6. Take one last look at the script. 7. Leave your dressing room. 8. Go on stage. The curtain is about to go up!

GROUP ACTIVITIES

1. Classifying

a. Have students name as many things/people from the pictures as they can for each of the following categories: people on the stage, clothes to wear on the stage, things on or near the stage, things in the dressing room, musical instruments with strings, musical instruments you blow into.

b. Have students group the words (except for musical instruments) into two categories: things that are important *before* the show and things that are important *during* the show.

Example:
before: sewing machine, makeup, dressing room, script
during: audience, spotlight, curtain, costume

2. Pantomime

Have students pantomime being the performers in the pictures, including playing the musical instruments. Have the rest of the group guess the performer or object being pantomimed. Extend the activity by using the pantomimes to introduce verbs related to the objects. Encourage the class to answer in complete sentences. Example: She's a dancer. She's singing. He's playing the piano. She's putting on makeup.

3. Talent Show

Have students put on a talent show in the target language. Teach the class or groups of students songs in the target language to present. (You might want to choose songs that students can act out.) Help groups of students write funny dialogues in the target language to include in the show. They might use situations they have studied with the transparencies and/or picture dictionary as the basis for the dialogues. Some possible situations are finding a mysterious trunk in an attic or meeting a talking snowman.

WRITING

Have students do these activities independently or as whole-class or group activities.

1. Write about what you could do for a talent show.
2. Write an article for a school newspaper about a talent show you have attended. *(Students could describe their talent show from Group Activity 3.)*
3. Write an article about an imaginary show. Which singers/actors/dancers would be in your show? What would they perform?

FOCUS ON LANGUAGE

The vocabulary in the unit contains several nouns that are made from verbs by the addition of a suffix; for example, in English, *sing—singer, dance—dancer*. Have students identify the words and verbs that are the roots. Have students list as many other nouns that contain the same suffix as they can.

VOCABULARY

The Talent Show	Le spectacle	El espectáculo	Der Wettbewerb	La mostra dei talenti
actor	l'acteur	el actor	der Schauspieler	l'attore
auditorium	la salle	el auditorio	die Aula	l'auditorio
stage	la scène	el escenario	die Bühne	il palcoscenico
scenery	le décor	el decorado	die Kulisse	il scenario
spotlight	le spot	el proyector de teatro	der Scheinwerfer	il fascio di luce
rope	la corde	la cuerda	das Seil	la corda
microphone	le microphone	el micrófono	das Mikrofon	il microfono
makeup	le maquillage	el maquillaje	die Schminke	il trucco
sheet music	les partitions	la música	die Noten	le carte di musica
conductor	le chef d'orchestre	el director	der Dirigent	il direttore d'orchestra
trumpet	la trompette	la trompeta	die Trompete	la tromba
piano	le piano	el piano	das Klavier	il pianoforte
actress	l'actrice	la actriz	die Schauspielerin	l'attrice
audience	les spectateurs	el público	die Zuhörer	il pubblico
curtain	le rideau	el telón	der Vorhang	il sipario
script	le texte	el guión	das Drehbuch	il copione
dressing room	la loge	el camarín	das Ankleidezimmer	il camerino
sewing machine	la machine à coudre	la máquina de coser	die Nähmaschine	la macchina per cucire
master of ceremonies	le maître des cérémonies	el animador	der Programmleiter	il cerimoniere
orchestra pit	la fosse d'orchestre	el foso de la orquesta	der Orchesterraum	la buca dell'orchestra
orchestra	l'orchestre	la orquesta	das Orchester	l'orchestra
accordion	l'accordéon	el acordeón	das Akkordeon	la fisarmonica
saxophone	le saxophone	el saxofón	das Saxophon	il sassofono
xylophone	le xylophone	el xilófono	das Xylophon	il silofono
children	les enfants	los niños	die Kinder	i ragazzi
singer	le chanteur	el cantante	der Sänger	il cantante
dancer	la danseuse	la bailarina	die Tänzerin	la ballerina
ballet slippers	les chaussons de danse	las zapatillas de ballet	die Tanzschuhe	le scarpette da ballo
tutu	le tutu	el tutú	das Tanzkostüm	il tutù
leotard	le maillot	la malla	das Trikot	la calzamaglia
costume	le costume	el disfraz	das Kostüm	il costume

mask	le masque	la máscara	die Maske	la maschera
wig	la perruque	la peluca	die Perücke	la parrucca
cymbals	les cymbales	los címbalos	die Becken	i piatti
French Lorn	le cor d'harmonie	el corno francés	das Waldhorn	il cornetto
violin	le violon	el violín	die Geige	il violino
bow	l'archet	el arco	der Bogen	l'archetto
guitar	la guitare	la guitarra	die Guitarre	la chitarra
drum	le tambour	el tambor	die Trommel	il tamburo
tuba	le tuba	la tuba	die Tuba	la tuba
flute	la flûte	la flauta	die Flöte	il flauto
trombone	le trombone	el trombón	die Posaune	il trombone
clarinet	la clarinette	el clarinete	die Klarinette	il clarinetto
cello	le violoncelle	el violoncelo	das Cello	il violoncello
strings	les cordes	las cuerdas	die Saiten	la corda
harp	la harpe	el arpa	die Harfe	l'arpa

20. At the Zoo

QUESTIONS ABOUT THE PICTURE

1. Name three animals that you see in or near the water in the picture.
2. Name two animals with long necks.
3. Which animal has a hump?
4. Which animals have spots?
5. Which animals are black and white?
6. *(right)* What is the gorilla doing?
7. *(center)* What is the zookeeper doing?
8. Which animals in the picture have babies?
9. Which animals are from the plains of Africa?
10. Which animals have you seen in a zoo?

ACTION STORIES

Possible topics: imitating animals, feeding animals

Example: Imitating animals

1. A kangaroo hops. Hop like a kangaroo. 2. An eagle flies. Fly like an eagle. 3. Elephants walk slowly from side to side. Walk like an elephant. 4. Lions roar. Roar like a lion. 5. Seals clap their flippers. Clap like a seal. 6. Parrots squawk. Squaw like a parrot.

GROUP ACTIVITIES

1. Classifying

Have students name as many animals from the picture as they can for each of the following categories: kinds of birds, kinds of bears, parts of a bird, animals that live in cold places, animals that live in hot places, kinds of cats, animals with spots, parts of a zebra, animals that could fit under a bed, animals that are bigger than you are.

2. Animal Descriptions

With the students, describe some of the animals. Write the following headings on the chalkboard: what the animal looks like, where the animal lives, what the animal eats, how the animal moves, what noise the animal makes. Have students call out answers for each heading, which you write on the chalkboard to make a chart. Once the chart is completed, have students orally provide two or three sentences for each animal. For example: A lion is a big cat. It has a mane and claws. It lives in Africa. It eats other animals on the plains. It can move quickly and pounce. It roars.

3. Debate

Present these instructions to the students:

> You can open a zoo for your school, but you can choose only ten animals to be in it. Which animals do you choose?

Have each student write down his or her choices. Have students compare their answers and defend their choices. At the end of the discussion, take a vote to see which ten animals should be in the zoo.

4. Interview

Have students role-play being a zookeeper. The rest of the class asks questions about the job such as: What is a typical day in your job? What do you like about your job? What don't you like about your job? Do you make a lot of money? Do you work long hours?

5. Discussion

Discuss with the students the question of what makes a good zoo. Is it a large number of animals? Is it seeing baby animals? Is it seeing animals in their natural homes?

WRITING

Have students do these activities independently or as whole-class or group activities.

1. List all the animals you have seen in a zoo.
2. Draw a make-believe animal. Use parts of other animals. Write the parts of the other animals you are using. Give your animal a name and describe it (e.g., where it lives, what it eats, how big it is, etc.)
3. Write about a trip to the zoo. What did you see? What did you like best?
4. Choose an animal and write about it. You might tell what group the animal belongs in, where the animal lives, what it eats, anything unusual about its habits.
5. You get one of the animals from the picture. What problems do you have taking care of it? What do you decide to do with it? Write the story.

FOCUS ON LANGUAGE

Animals come in many different sizes and have many different characteristics. Present/review the formation of the comparative in the target language. Then present comparatives such as the following and have students use them in sentences to compare animals:

bigger	smaller
faster	slower
noisier	taller
more powerful	more intelligent

VOCABULARY

At the Zoo	Au zoo	En el jardín zoológico	Im Zoo	Allo zoo
zookeeper	le gardien de zoo	el guardián de zoológico	der Tierpfleger	lo zoologo
rhinoceros	le rhinocéros	el rinoceronte	das Nashorn	il rinoceronte
lion	le lion	el león	der Löwe	il leone
tiger	le tigre	el tigre	der Tiger	la tigre
tiger cub	le petit tigre	el cachorro de tigre	das Tigerjunge	il tigrotto
jaguar	le jaguar	el jaguar	der Jaguar	il giaguaro
leopard	le léopard	el leopardo	der Leopard	il gattopardo
flamingo	le flamant	el flamenco	der Flamingo	il fenicottero
owl	le hibou	la lechuza	die Eule	il gufo
swan	le cygne	el cisne	der Schwan	il cigno
penguin	le pingouin	el pingüino	der Pinguin	il pinguino
peacock	le paon	el pavo real	der Pfau	il pavone
eagle	l'aigle	el águila	der Adler	l'aquila
elephant	l'éléphant	el elefante	der Elefant	l'elefante
ostrich	l'autruche	el avestruz	der Strauß	lo struzzo
bear	l'ours	el oso	der Bär	l'orso
bear cub	l'ourson	el cachorro de oso	das Bärchen	l'orsacchiotto
polar bear	l'ours blanc	el oso polar	der Eisbär	l'orso bianco
panda	le panda	el panda	der Panda	l'orso panda
gorilla	le gorille	el gorila	der Gorilla	il gorilla
parrot	le perroquet	el loro	der Papagei	il pappagallo
snake	le serpent	la serpiente	die Schlange	il serpente
seal	le phoque	la foca	die Robbe	la foca
walrus	le morse	la morsa	das Walroß	il tricheco
hump	la bosse	la giba	der Höcker	la gobba
camel	le chameau	el camello	das Kamel	il cammello
animals	les animaux	los animales	die Tiere	gli animali
fox	le renard	el zorro	der Fuchs	la volpe
wolf	le loup	el lobo	der Wolf	il lupo
alligator	l'alligator	el caimán	der Alligator	il coccodrillo
zebra	le zèbre	la cebra	das Zebra	la zebra

giraffe	la girafe	la jirafa	die Giraffe	la giraffa
monkey	le singe	el mono	der Affe	la scimmia
hippopotamus	le hippopotame	el hipopótamo	das Flußpferd	l'ippopotamo
kangaroo	le kangourou	el canguro	das Känguruh	il canguro
deer	la biche	el ciervo	das Reh	il cervo
lizard	le lézard	el lagarto	die Eidechse	la lucertola
turtle	la tortue	la tortuga	die Schildkröte	la tartaruga
horns	les cornes	los cuernos	die Hörner	le corna
wings	les ailes	las alas	die Flügel	le ali
feathers	les plumes	las plumas	die Federn	le piume
beak	le bec	el pico	der Schnabel	il becco
paw	la patte	la pata	die Tatze	la zampa
claws	les griffes	las garras	die Krallen	l'artiglio
mane	la crinière	la melena	die Mähne	la criniera
tail	la queue	la cola	der Schwanz	la coda
hoof	le sabot	el casco	der Huf	lo zoccolo
stripes	les rayures	las rayas	die Streifen	le striscie
spots	les taches	las manchas	die Flecken	le macchie

21. At the Circus

QUESTIONS ABOUT THE PICTURES

1. What are two performers you see at a circus?
2. What are three animals you see at a circus?
3. What does a trapeze artist do?
4. *(left picture—left)* What is the man in the booth doing?
5. *(left picture—center)* Describe the clown in the center of the picture.
6. *(left picture—bottom)* Tell what the people are doing.
7. *(right picture)* Describe the inside of the circus tent (how many rings, what is in the nearest ring, etc.).
8. What are some things that the clowns in a circus do?
9. Have you ever taken pictures with a camera? What kinds of pictures have you taken?
10. Have you ever been to the circus? What did you see?

ACTION STORIES

Possible topics: on your way to the circus, buying a ticket, taking a picture, being a clown

Example: On your way to the circus

1. Let's go to the circus. What a crowd! 2. Walk to the ticket booth. 3. Wait in line. 4. It's your turn. Say, "I'd like four tickets." 5. Give the person money. 6. Take your tickets. 7. Oh, there's an elephant. 8. Take a picture of it with your camera. Try to get the whole elephant in your picture. 9. Buy some popcorn. 10. Taste some. It's good!

GROUP ACTIVITIES

1. Classifying

Have students name as many things from the picture as they can for each of the following categories: people in the circus, animals in the circus, things to eat at the circus, places at the circus, things an acrobat does, things a lion tamer uses, things a tightrope walker uses, things for a camera.

2. Pantomime

Have students pantomime doing activities related to the circus: being a tightrope walker, a clown walking on stilts, etc. Have the rest of the group guess the act and the objects being used. Extend the activity by using the pantomimes to introduce the verbs that go with the objects, encouraging the class to answer in complete sentences. Example: She's a trapeze artist. She's swinging from trapeze to trapeze high above the rings.

3. Debate

Present the following questions to the group: What is the most dangerous job in the circus? What is the most exciting act in the circus? Have each student write down his or her answers. Have students compare their answers and defend their choices. At the end of the discussion, take a vote to see which acts are considered the most dangerous or the most exciting.

4. Interview

Have students role-play being a circus performer. The rest of the class asks questions about the job such as: What is a typical day in your job? What do you like about your job? What don't you like about your job? Do you make a lot of money? Do you work long hours? Is your job dangerous? What special things do you need to do your job?

WRITING

Have students do these activities independently or as whole-class or group activities.

1. List at least ten things you might see in a circus parade.
2. List at least ten things you might see inside a circus tent.
3. Make an ad for a circus. Try to make people want to come to see your circus. Tell about some of the attractions, and include a drawing.
4. Write a story about a clown in the circus. For example, you can write about the busiest, happiest clown in the circus.
5. Write a make-believe or true story about a visit to the circus.

FOCUS ON LANGUAGE

The circus, the greatest show on earth, is a place for superlatives. Present/review the formation of the superlative in the target language. Then present superlatives such as the following, and have students use them in sentences:

the biggest	the funniest
the most dangerous	the most exciting
the bravest	the tallest

VOCABULARY

At the Circus	Au cirque	En el circo	Im Zirkus	Al circo
clown	le clown	la payasa	der Clown	il pagliaccio
popcorn	le pop-corn	las palomitas	das Popkorn	il popcorn
caramel apple	la pomme enrobée de caramel	la manzana de caramelo	der kandierte Apfel	la mela caramellata
balloon	le ballon	el globo	der Luftballon	il pallone
peanuts	les cacahuètes	los cacahuates	die Erdnüsse	le arachidi
film	la pellicule	la película	der Film	la pellicola
magician	le magicien	el mago	der Zauberer	il mago
lion	le lion	el león	der Löwe	il leone
tent pole	le mât de tente	el palo de tienda	die Zeltstange	l'asta della tenda
elephant	l'éléphant	el elefante	der Elefant	l'elefante
flashbulb	le flash	la lámpara flash	das Blitzlicht	il riflettore
camera	l'appareil-photo	la cámara	die Kamera	la macchina fotografica
juggler	le jongleur	el malabarista	der Jongleur	il giocoliere
tickets	les tickets	las entradas	die Eintrittskarten	i biglietti
baton	le bâton	la vara	der Stab	il battone
turban	le turban	el turbante	der Turban	il turbano
lightbulb	l'ampoule	la bombilla	die Glühbirne	la lampadina
night	la nuit	la noche	die Nacht	la notte
ticket booth	le guichet	la taquilla	die Kartenverkaufstelle	la biglietteria
stilts	les échasses	los zancos	die Stelzen	i trampoli
big top	le grand chapiteau	la tienda mayor del circo	das Zirkuszelt	la tenda
circus parade	la parade de cirque	el desfile del circo	die Zirkusparade	la parata di circo
rest rooms	les toilettes	los baños	die Toilette	i gabinetti
bareback rider	la cavalière qui monte à cru	la jinete	die sattellose Reiterin	la cavallerizza senza sella
trapeze	le trapèze	el trapecio	das Trapez	il trapezio
trapeze artist	le trapéziste	el trapecista	der Trapezkünstler	il trapezista
band	les musiciens	la banda	das Orchester	la banda
whip	le fouet	el látigo	die Peitsche	la frusta
lion tamer	le dompteur de lions	el domador de fieras	der Löwenzähmer	il domatore dei leoni
tightrope walker	la funambule	la gimnasta de la cuerda floja	die Drahtseilkünstlerin	la funambola

tightrope	la corde raide	la cuerda floja	das Drahtseil	la corda tesa per funamboli
cage	la cage	la jaula	der Käfig	la gabbia
safety net	le filet de protection	la red de seguridad	das Sicherheitsnetz	la rete di sicurezza
unicycle	le monocycle	el monociclo	das Einrad	l'uniciclo
handstand	faire l'arbre droit	el farol	der Handstand	la verticale
acrobat	l'acrobate	el acróbata	der Artist	l'acrobata
ring	la piste	la pista de circo	die Manege	l'arena
hoop	le cerceau	el aro	der Reifen	il cerchio
rope ladder	l'échelle de corde	la escalera de cuerda	die Seilleiter	la scala per arrampicarsi
rope	la corde	la cuerda	das Seil	la corda
headstand	faire le poirier	la parada de cabeza	der Kopfstand	la verticale sulla testa
somersault	la culbute	el salto mortal	der Purzelbaum	il salto mortale
cartwheel	faire la roue	la voltereta lateral	das Rad	la ruota di carretta
cotton candy	la barbe à papa	el algodón de azúcar	die Zuckerwatte	lo zucchero filato
cape	la cape	la capa	das Cape	la mantellina
ringmaster	Monsieur Loyal	el maestro de ceremonias	der Zirkusdirektor	il presentatore

22. In the Ocean

QUESTIONS ABOUT THE PICTURE

1. Whom do you see in the picture?
2. What vehicle do you see underwater?
3. What things (not animals) do you see on the bottom of the ocean?
4. What animals do you see on the bottom of the ocean?
5. What animals do you see floating in the ocean?
6. What is the scuba diver doing? What is the snorkeler doing?
7. What is the person in the boat doing?
8. Why does the scuba diver have flippers/an oxygen tank/a mask?
9. What are the different classes of animals in the picture?
10. Have you ever been to the ocean/beach? What did you see there?

ACTION STORIES

Possible topics: a scuba diver getting ready to dive, a trip to the bottom of the ocean, being a snorkeler

Example: Being a snorkeler

1. Be a snorkeler. 2. Put on your flippers—left foot, right foot. 3. Put on your snorkel and your mask. 4. Go to the beach and dive into the water. 5. Swim and look down. 6. Try to catch one of the fish that are swimming by. 7. Go down to the coral reef. 8. Pick up a shell. 9. Go back to the surface of the ocean. 10. Take off your mask and breathe the air.

GROUP ACTIVITIES

1. Classifying

Have students name as many things from the picture as they can for each of the following categories: things for a scuba diver to wear, kinds of treasure, things that have to do with a shipwreck, things on an ocean beach, parts of a fish, fish in the ocean, animals (not fish) in the ocean.

2. Guessing Game: Location

You or a student describes the location of an object in the picture, and other students name the object being described. Have students use the equivalent of the prepositions *next to, in front of, in back of, on, in, below, above* . Example: It's next to the shark. It's above the school of fish. *(sea turtle)*

3. Chain Story

Have students play a chain game in which each student adds one sentence to a group story, repeating what was previously said. The sentences should tell about what they saw on a trip to the bottom of the ocean. Example: I went down to the bottom of the ocean. First I saw a dolphin. Next I saw an octopus, etc.

4. Debate

Present this situation to students:

> Your class is in charge of starting an aquarium for your school. But for now you can only have six different kinds of animals. Which do you choose?

Have each student write down his or her answers. Have students compare their answers and defend their choices. At the end of the discussion, take a vote to see which animals are to be included.

5. Interview

Have students role-play being a scuba diver. The rest of the class asks questions about the job such as: What do you see on your trips? What do you like about scuba diving? What don't you like about it? Is it dangerous?

WRITING

Have students do these activities independently or as whole-class or group activities.

1. List some animals that you would see in an aquarium.
2. You are the scuba diver in the picture. Tell your friends what you saw on your trip to the ocean bottom.
3. You are the scuba diver in the picture. You were going to bring back to the surface the treasure you have in your hands. But something happened so that you couldn't do that. Tell the story of what happened.

4. Tell about a trip to the aquarium.
5. Tell about a trip to the beach.

FOCUS ON LANGUAGE

With the students, prepare a word association listing words that are related to water. Have students illustrate the words.

Examples:

verbs: swim, sink, float, splash

bodies of water: ocean, lake, river, pond

other related words: beach, wave

VOCABULARY

In the Ocean	L'océan	En el mar	Im Ozean	L'oceano
scuba diver	le plongeur sous-marin	el buceador	der Taucher	il tuffatore subacqueo
wet suit	la combinaison de plongée	el traje de goma	der Wasseranzug	la muta
flipper	la palme	la aleta	die Schwimmflosse	la pinna
oxygen tank	le ballon d'oxygène	el tanque de oxígeno	der Lufttank	l'autorespiratore
snorkel	le tube pour masque sous-marin	el esnórquel	der Schnorchel	il boccaglio
mask	le masque	la máscara	die Tauchermaske	la maschera
starfish	l'étoile de mer	la estrella de mar	der Seestern	la stella di mare
jellyfish	la méduse	la medusa	die Qualle	la medusa
sea turtle	la tortue marine	la tortuga de mar	die Seeschildkröte	la tartaruga di mare
lobster	le homard	la langosta	der Hummer	l'aragosta
stingray	la pastenague	la pastinaca	der Stachelfisch	la razza
dolphin	le dauphin	el delfín	der Delphin	il delfino
shark	le requin	el tiburón	der Haifisch	lo squalo
octopus	le poulpe	el pulpo	der Seepolyp	il polpo
tentacle	le tentacule	el tentáculo	der Fühlarm	il tentacolo
swordfish	l'espadon	el pez espada	der Schwertfisch	il pesce spada
angelfish	l'ange	el angelote	der Engelfisch	il pesce angelo
school (of fish)	le banc de poissons	el banco	der Zug	il banco
fishing line	la ligne de pêche	el hilo de pesar	die Angelschnur	la lenza
fishhook	le hameçon	el anzuelo	der Angelhaken	l'amo
buoy	la bouée	la boya	die Boje	il gavitello
submarine	le sous-marin	el submarino	das Unterseeboot	il sommergibile
porthole	le hublot	la portilla	die Luke	l'oblò
sea urchin	l'oursin	el erizo marino	der Seeigel	il riccio di mare
sea horse	l'hippocampe	el hipocampo	das Seepferdchen	il cavallo di mare
seaweed	les algues	el alga marina	der Seetang	l'alga marina
shipwreck	l'épave	el naufragio	der Schiffbruch	il relitto di nave naufragio
helm	la barre	el timón	der Helm	l'elmo
cannon	le canon	el cañón	die Kanone	il cannone
anchor	l'ancre	la ancla	der Anker	l'ancora

treasure chest	le trésor	el arca de tesoro	die Schatzkiste	il cassetone
treasure	le trésor	el tesoro	der Schatz	il tesoro
gold	l'or	el oro	das Gold	l'oro
silver	l'argent	la plata	das Silber	l'argento
jewel	le bijou	la joya	das Juwel	il gioiello
barnacle	la bernache	el percebe	die Entenmuschel	il lupo di mare
coral	le corail	el coral	die Koralle	il corallo
coral reef	le récif de corail	el arrecife de coral	das Korallenriff	il banco corallifero
seashell	le coquillage	la concha de mar	die Muschel	la conchiglia
wave	la vague	la ola	die Welle	l'onda
sand	le sable	la arena	der Sand	la sabbia
bubble	la bulle	la burbuja	die Blase	il gorgoglio
scales	les écailles	las escamas	die Schuppen	le scaglie
gills	les ouïes	las agallas	die Kiemen	le branchie
fin	la nageoire	la aleta	die Flosse	la pinna
clam	la palourde	la almeja	die Muschel	l'ostrica
crab	le crabe	el cangrejo	die Krabbe	il granchio
squid	le calmar	el calamar	der Tintenfisch	il calamaro
whale	la baleine	la ballena	der Wal	la balena

23. Space

QUESTIONS ABOUT THE PICTURE

1. What things does an astronaut wear?
2. What things do you see on the surface of the planet?
3. What vehicles do you see in the back of the picture?
4. What else do you see in the back of the picture?
5. *(upper right)* What are the scientists doing?
6. Where are the astronauts? What are they doing?
7. What is a space station/landing capsule/lunar rover used for?
8. Why do astronauts need to wear space suits?
9. What is the center of the solar system? What does the earth move around? What does the moon move around?
10. Would you like to travel in space? Why or why not?

ACTION STORIES

Possible topics: taking a trip to the moon, taking a trip through outer space, doing a science experiment

Example: Doing a science experiment

1. Do a science experiment. 2. Go to the laboratory. 3. Put on your lab coat. 4. Take out the beakers from the refrigerator. 5. Pour some blue liquid into a test tube. 6. Shake the test tube. 7. Look! Big red bubbles are coming out. 8. Pour the liquid down the sink!

GROUP ACTIVITIES

1. Classifying

Have students name as many things from the picture as they can for each of the following categories: vehicles in space, things an astronaut wears, parts of the solar system, things you see in space, things you might see on the moon, things a scientist uses.

2. Order of Events

Write the following events on the board, mixing up their order. Have students write them in the order in which they would occur. A trip to the moon: get on the rocket with the spaceship from Earth, circle the moon, get on the landing capsule, get in the lunar rover, ride around the moon, return to the landing capsule, return to the spaceship, return to Earth.

3. Discussion

Discuss the items in the picture so that students understand the meaning of such terms as: galaxy, constellation, asteroids, and solar system.

4. Interview

Have individual students role-play being an astronaut. The rest of the class asks questions about the job such as: What do you see on your trips? What do you like about your job? What don't you like about it? Is it dangerous?

WRITING

Have students do these activities independently or as whole-class or group activities.

1. Draw a series of pictures showing a trip to the moon. You can include the space ship taking off, the ship going from the Earth to the moon, the landing capsule landing on the moon, the astronauts on a lunar rover on the moon. On the pictures, write the names of all the objects that you can.
2. Draw a picture of the solar system. Label the sun, Earth, the moon, and any other planets you can.
3. You have taken a trip in the lunar rover on the moon. Tell what you saw.
4. You are an astronaut who is the first to go to the planet where no one has ever been. Tell about your trip.
5. You are about to take a walk on the moon. There are no cameras. You have to tell the mission control on Earth what you are doing at every moment. Write the dialogue between you and mission control. Use sentences such as "Now I'm walking down the ladder" and "Now I see a crater."

FOCUS ON LANGUAGE

With the students, prepare a word association listing things that an astronaut does. Have students illustrate the words: get into the space ship, take off, orbit, land, float in the space ship, take a space walk, do science experiments, eat packaged food, etc.

VOCABULARY

Space	**L'espace**	**El espacio**	**Der Weltraum**	**Lo spazio**
astronaut	l'astronaute	el astronauta	der Raumfahrer	l'astronauta
footprint	l'empreinte de pied	la huella del pie	die Fußstapfe	l'orma
space shuttle	la navette spatiale	el vuelo espacial	der Raumflugkörper	la navicella spaziale
cargo bay	la soute	el compartimiento de flete	der Frachtraum	la merce imbarcata
control panel	le tableau de bord	el tablero de control	die Kontrolltafel	il pannello di controllo
satellite	le satellite	el satélite	der Trabant	il satellite
spaceship	la soucoupe volante	el platillo volante	das Raumschiff	l'astronave
alien	l'extra-terrestre	el extraterrestre	der Fremdling	l'extraterreste
antenna	l'antenne	la antena	die Antenne	l'antenna
asteroid	l'astéroïde	el asteroide	der Asteroid	l'asteroide
space suit	le scaphandre de cosmonaute	el traje espacial	der Raumanzug	la tuta spaziale
space walk	la marche dans l'espace	el caminar en el espacio	die Raumwanderung	il passeggio nello spazio
lunar rover	la jeep lunaire	el rover lunar	das Mondfahrzeug	la macchina lunare
landing capsule	la capsule d'atterrissage	la cápsula de aterrizaje	das Landungsgerät	la capsula spaziale
ladder	l'échelle	la escalera	die Leiter	la scala a pioli
space station	la station spatiale	la estación espacial	die Raumstation	la stazione spaziale
solar panel	le panneau solaire	el tablero solar	die Sonnenzellen	il pannello solare
meteor shower	la pluie de météores	la lluvia meteórica	der Sternschnuppen-schwarm	la pioggia dei meteori
constellation	la constellation	la constelación	das Sternbild	la costellazione
solar system	le système solaire	el sistema solar	das Sonnensystem	il sistema solare
space helmet	le casque d'astronaute	el casco espacial	der Raumhelm	l'elmo spaziale
moon rock	la pierre de lune	la piedra de luna	der Mondfels	il cristallo di luna
laboratory	le laboratoire	el laboratorio	das Labor	il laboratorio
scientist	le savant	el científico	der Naturwissenschaftler	lo scienziato
lab coat	la blouse de laboratorie	la bata de laboratorio	der Labormantel	il camice
microscope	le microscope	el microscopio	das Mikroskop	il microscopio
computer	l'ordinateur	la computadora	der Komputer	il computer
beaker	le vase à bec	la probeta	das Becherglas	l'alambicco
test tube	l'éprouvette	el tubo de ensayo	das Reagenzglas	la provetta

galaxy	la galaxie	la galaxia	die Milchstraße	la galassia
Earth	la terre	la Tierra	die Erde	la Terra
the moon	la lune	la luna	der Mond	la luna
the sun	le soleil	el sol	die Sonne	il sole
planet	la planète	la planeta	der Planet	il pianeta
rings	les anneaux	los anillos	die Höfe	i circoli
crater	le cratère	el cráter	der Krater	il cratere
stars	les étoiles	las estrellas	die Sterne	le stelle
comet	la comète	el cometa	der Komet	la cometa
nebula	la nébuleuse	la nebulosa	der Nebelfleck	la nebulosa
rocket	la fusée interplanétaire	el cohete	die Rakete	il missile
robot	l'automate	el robot	der Roboter	il robot

24. Human History

QUESTIONS ABOUT THE PICTURE

1. The picture shows life on Earth many thousands of years ago. Name four animals that you can no longer find on Earth.
2. Name two tools that the people could use.
3. How did the people in the picture get food?
4. In what places did the people in the picture live?
5. What did the people in the picture wear?
6. What are the people at the bottom of the picture doing?
7. What are the people at the right of the picture doing?
8. Why are the people at the right of the picture more advanced?
9. What dangers or problems did the people in the picture have?
10. Name some things that people in the picture did not have that we have.

ACTION STORIES

Possible topics: be a cave dweller, be a village dweller

Example: Be a village dweller

1. Be a village dweller. 2. Go by the fire and warm your hands. 3. Go to the well. 4. Get a bucket and fill it with water. 5. Take the bucket to the village. 6. Pet the dog on the way. 7. Go by the weaver. 8. Help her weave on the loom. 9. Get a basket of wheat. 10. Take it back to the hut.

GROUP ACTIVITIES

1. Classifying

Have students name as many things from the picture as they can for each of the following categories: animals you no longer see, things to use for hunting, things to wear, places to live, things people make, things that people grow to eat.

2. Ways People Lived

Discuss with students what the picture illustrates: it shows how people lived thousands of years ago. Point out that the people at the left lived at an earlier time than the people at the right. The people at the right had more inventions that made their lives easier. The people at the left were cave dwellers. The people at the right were village dwellers. Help students complete this chart, using the information in the picture:

	Cave dwellers	Village dwellers
where people lived	,	
what people wore	,	
what people ate	,	
what tools people used	,	
what animals people saw	,	
what inventions people had	,	

3. Discussion

Have students discuss how our lives differ from the life of the people in the picture. Have students list things in these categories: inventions we have that the people in the picture did not have, dangers people in the picture had/dangers we have, where people lived/where we live, how the people got food/how we get food.

WRITING

Have students do these activities independently or as whole-class or group activities.

1. List things in the picture that you don't see today.
2. List things in the picture that you see today.
3. You have traveled in the past to the place in the picture, but no one else in your class has. Write about what you saw.
4. You are a cave dweller or a village dweller. Write about your day-to-day life.

FOCUS ON LANGUAGE

Some scientists think that the first languages developed by our ancestors came out of the use of sounds with gestures. Tell students that we still use gestures to communicate. Teach students some common gestures used in the target culture. Here are some possibilities: hello, good-bye, come here, I don't know, I can't believe it, stop.

VOCABULARY

Human History	L'histoire humaine	La historia de la humanidad	Menschheitsgeschichte	La storia humana
rock	la roche	la piedra	der Felsen	la roccia
boulder	le bloc de pierre	la roca	der Felsblock	il masso
bone	l'os	el hueso	der Knochen	l'osso
insect	l'insecte	el insecto	das Insekt	l'insetto
fern	la fougère	el helecho	der Farn	la felce
tree	l'arbre	el árbol	der Baum	l'albero
cave	la caverne	la caverna	die Höhle	la caverna
fur	la fourrure	la piel	der Pelz	la pelliccia
fire	le feu	el fuego	das Feuer	il fuoco
stick	le bâton	el palo	der Stock	il bastoncino
wheel	la roue	la rueda	das Rad	la ruota
flint	le silex	el pedernal	der Feuerstein	la selce
arrowhead	la pointe de flèche	la punta de flecha	die Pfeilspitze	la punta di freccia
club	la massue	el palo	die Keule	il bastone
spear	la lance	la lanza	der Speer	la lancia
mammoth	le mammouth	el mamut	das Mammut	il mammùt
tusk	la défense	el colmillo	der Stoßzahn	la zanna
trunk	la trompe	la trompa	der Rüssel	la proboscide
bison	le bison	el bisonte	der Bison	il bisonte
paint	la peinture	la pintura	die Farbe	il colore
cave drawing	le dessin des cavernes	el dibujo de caverna	die Höhlenmalerei	il disegno di caverna
hut	la hutte	la cabaña	die Hütte	la capanna
corn	le maïs	el maíz	der Mais	il granturco
wheat	le blé	el trigo	der Weizen	il grano
weaver	la tisserande	la tejedora	der Weber	la tessitrice
loom	le métier à tisser	el telar	der Webstuhl	il telaio
kiln	le four	el horno	der Brennofen	la fornace
potter	le potier	el alfarero	der Töpfer	il vasaio
pot	le pot	el pote	der Topf	il vaso
clay	l'argile	el barro	der Lehm	l'argilla

cart	la charrette	la carreta	der Karren	il carro
basket	le panier	la canasta	der Korb	la cesta
leather	le cuir	el cuero	das Leder	il cuoio
fishing	la pêche	la pesca	das Fischen	la pesca
hunter	le chasseur	el cazador	der Jäger	il cacciatore
well	le puits	el pozo	der Ziehbrunnen	il pozzo
bucket	le seau	el balde	der Eimer	la secchia
water	l'eau	el agua	das Wasser	l'acqua
cloth	la toile	la tela	das Tuch	il panno
saber-toothed tiger	le tigre préhistorique	el tigre de dientes de sable	der Säbelzahntiger	la tigre preistorica
crop	la récolte	la cosecha	die Ernte	la raccolta
field	le champ	el campo	das Feld	il campo
village	le village	la villa	das Dorf	il villaggio
cave dwellers	les habitants des cavernes	los cavernícolas	die Höhlenbewohner	gli abitatori di caverne
skeleton	le squelette	el esqueleto	das Skelett	lo scheletro
dinosaur	le dinosaure	el dinosaurio	der Dinosaurier	il dinosauro
pterodactyl	le ptérodactyle	el pterodáctilo	der Flugsaurier	il pterodattilo

25. The Make-Believe Castle

QUESTIONS ABOUT THE PICTURE

1. What places do you see in the picture?
2. What does a knight wear?
3. Name three magical creatures in the picture.
4. Who are entertaining the king and queen?
5. What does a blacksmith make? What tools does a blacksmith use?
6. Name three weapons that a knight uses.
7. What is a saddle/reins/stirrups used for?
8. Describe the giant/the elf/the dragon.
9. What things in the picture might have existed many hundreds of years ago? What things exist only in stories?
10. Would you like to visit the castle in the picture? Why or why not?

ACTION STORIES

Possible topics: getting on a horse, entering a castle, be a knight

Example: Ride a horse

1. Go to the stable. 2. Pet your horse. 3. Give it an apple to eat. 4. Put the saddle on the horse. 5. Put a bridle on the horse. 6. Get up onto the horse. 7. Put your feet into the stirrups. 8. Get ready for a ride through the forest!

GROUP ACTIVITIES

1. Classifying

Have students name as many things from the picture as they can for each of the following categories: people, animals, places, tools, magical people and things.

2. Chain Story

Have students play a chain game in which each student adds one sentence to a group story, repeating what was previously said. The sentences should tell about what they saw on a trip through the castle. Example: I went to the make-believe castle. First I crossed the drawbridge. Then I saw a knight. Next I saw a queen. Then I saw a minstrel singing.

3. Discussion

a. Many things and people in the picture exist only in fairy tales. With students, list and describe these creatures:

elf: small, likes to do tricks

fairy: can do magic things, often has a magic wand, can be good or bad

dragon: breathes fire, fights knights

giants: huge creatures, can be good or bad

b. With advanced students, have students tell about fairy tales in which these creatures appear.

4. Group Story

Write a group story about one of the magical creatures in the picture: the dragon, the giant, the elf, the fairy. Prompt students with questions such as the following: Is the creature good or bad? Why is the creature at the castle? Does it want to help or hurt the people at the castle?

WRITING

Have students do these activities independently or as whole-class or group activities.

1. List things in the picture that you don't see today.
2. List things in the picture that you see today.
3. You have traveled in the past to the place in the picture, but no one else in your class has. Write about what you saw.
4. You are a king or queen in the past. Design your own castle. Write about what it is like. You may want to draw a picture of it. Label the things you put in your picture.
5. Write a story with a magical creature. For example, it might be a magical spider that spins golden webs.

FOCUS ON LANGUAGE

The imaginary castle is set in the past. While it has magical creatures that don't exist, it also doesn't have many things that we have today. Have students practice negative forms by describing things that the castle doesn't have.

Examples:

The castle doesn't have electric lights.

The minstrel doesn't have an electric guitar.

The king can't watch television.

VOCABULARY

The Make-Believe Castle	Le château de fantaisie	El castillo de ficción	das Märchenschloß	Il castello immaginato
banner	la bannière	el estandarte	das Banner	lo stendardo
dragon	le dragon	el dragón	der Drache	il drago
magic wand	la baguette magique	la varilla mágica	der Zauberstab	la bacchetta magica
fairy	la fée	el hada	die Fee	la maga
elf	le lutin	el duende	der Elf	l'elfo
giant	le géant	el gigante	der Riese	il gigante
forge	la forge	la fragua	die Schmiede	la fornace
blacksmith	le forgeron	el herrero	der Hufschmied	il fabbro ferraio
anvil	l'enclume	el yunque	der Amboß	l'incudine
horseshoe	le fer à cheval	la herradura	das Hufeisen	il ferro di cavallo
tower	la tour	la torre	der Turm	la torre
courtyard	la cour	el patio	der Hof	il cortile
squire	l'écuyer	el escudero	der Edelknabe	lo scudiero
knight	le chevalier	el caballero	der Ritter	il cavaliere
armor	l'armure	la armadura	die Rüstung	la corazza
chain mail	la cotte de mailles	la cota de mallas	der Kettenpanzer	la maglia di ferro
forest	la forêt	el bosque	der Wald	la foresta
saddle	la selle	la silla de montar	der Sattel	la sella
stirrup	l'étrier	el estribo	der Steigbügel	la staffa
reins	les rênes	las riendas	die Zügel	le briglie
stable	l'écurie	el establo	der Stall	la stalla
dungeon	le donjon	el calabozo	der Kerker	il carcere sotterraneo
moat	les douves	el foso	der Wallgraben	il fosso
castle	le château	el castillo	das Schloß	il castello
court jester	le fou	el bufón	der Hofnarr	il burlone
minstrel	le troubadour	el trovador	der Minnesänger	il menestrello
unicorn	la licorne	el unicornio	das Einhorn	l'unicorno
lance	la lance	la lanza	die Lanze	la lancia
shield	l'écu	el escudo	der Schild	lo scudo
ax	la hache	el hacha	das Beil	l'accetta
sword	l'épée	la espada	das Schwert	la spada

bow	l'arc	el arco	der Bogen	l'arco
arrow	la flèche	la flecha	der Pfeil	la freccia
quiver	le carquois	la aljaba	der Köcher	la faretra
archer	l'archer	el arquero	der Bogenschütze	l'arciere
drawbridge	le pont-levis	el puente levadizo	die Zugbrücke	il ponte levatoio
bat	la chauve-souris	el murciélago	die Fledermaus	il pipistrello
rat	le rat	la rata	die Ratte	il ratto
crown	la couronne	la corona	die Krone	la corona
king	le roi	el rey	der König	il re
queen	la reine	la reina	die Königin	la regina
princess	la princesse	la princesa	die Prinzessin	la principessa
prince	le prince	el príncipe	der Prinz	il principe
throne	le trône	el trono	der Thron	il trono
spider	l'araignée	la araña	die Spinne	il ragno
spiderweb	la toile d'araignée	la telaraña	die Spinnwebe	la ragnatela

26. The Mouse Hunt (Prepositions and Adjectives)

QUESTIONS ABOUT THE PICTURE

1. *(upper left)* What is the mouse on top of? What is the mouse under? What is the mouse in front of?
2. What is the opposite of *inside/tall*?
3. What thing in the picture is *old/new*?
4. What thing in the picture is *sharp*?
5. What thing in the picture is *hot/cold*? What other things can be hot/cold?
6. What thing is soft in the picture? What other things can be soft?
7. *(top right)* What is the *fast/slow* mouse doing?
8. *(center top)* How is the mouse being *bad*?
9. How do you feel after you are out in the rain? (*wet*)
10. What things make you feel happy?

ACTION STORIES

Possible topic: following directions with prepositions

Prepositions: Students should have some small objects and a small box or other enclosed object to work with. Give students series of directions for placing the objects.

Examples: Place the red pencil *inside* the box. Put the black pencil *under* the box.

GROUP ACTIVITIES

1. Opposites

Prepare several sets of word cards with word pairs that are opposites. Each card should have one word or phrase on it. You might want to prepare the cards together with the students. Mix up the sets of cards. Give a set to each group of students. They are to group the opposites together.

Examples: in front of/behind, far/near, etc.

2. Words in Context/Chanting

With the students, prepare sentences that illustrate the meaning of the opposite sets. Things in the environment can be used.

Examples: The flag is behind the teacher's desk./The bookcase is in front of the teacher's desk. The globe is heavy./A paper clip is light. Make up chants based on the sentences for students to respond. Example: The globe is heavy, heavy, heavy. The paper clip is light, light, light.

3. Memory Game

Put several objects (e.g., pencils, notebooks, clips, toys) on a desk or some place where the class/group can see them. Position the objects to illustrate the various prepositions in the picture. Tell students that they should try to remember the positions of objects and give them a few minutes to study their location. Then have students see how many locations they can remember. You might prompt them with questions (What was on the red notebook?) or with a list of objects whose position they should identify. Determine which individual/group has the most items correct.

4. Group Discussion

With the students, list as many nouns as you can for the adjectives in the unit.

Examples: *left:* shoe, hand, glove; *light:* feather, package, book; *open:* door, box, envelope

5. Group Story

With the class, prepare a story about two people or animals who like opposite things.

Example: Happy Mouse is *small*. It sleeps on a *soft* bed. It likes to sleep with the light *on*. It likes a cup of *hot* milk before going to sleep. Sad Mouse is *large*. It sleeps on a *hard* bed. It likes to sleep with the light *off*. It likes a glass of *cold* milk before going to sleep.

You might want the students to continue the story by telling what happens when the two people or animals go on a trip together.

WRITING

Have students do these activities independently or as whole-class or group activities.

1. Make a preposition book. Draw pictures to illustrate words that tell where things are, such as *behind, above*. Label each picture with the words.
2. Make an adjective book. Draw pictures to illustrate words that describe things, such as *old, new, clean, dirty*.

FOCUS ON LANGUAGE

With students, prepare lists of adjectives to describe nouns. Here are some nouns to describe: a cat, a baby, a bedroom, a road.

VOCABULARY

The Mouse Hunt	La chasse aux souris	A la caza del ratón	Die Mäusejagd	La caccia dei topi
under	sous	debajo de	unter	sotto
above	au-dessus de	sobre	über	sopra
up	en haut	arriba	oben	in su
down	en bas	abajo	unten	in giù
on top of	sur	encima de	auf	su
next to	à côté de	al lado de	neben	vicino a
in front of	devant	enfrente de	vor	davanti
behind	derrière	detrás de	hinter	dietro
top	le haut	de arriba	das Oberteil	la cima
bottom	le bas	de abajo	die Unterseite	il fondo
inside	à l'intérieur	dentro de	innerhalb	indietro
outside	à l'extérieur	fuera de	außerhalb	fuori
near	près	cerca de	nah	vicino
far	loin	lejos de	fern	lontano
between	entre	entre	zwischen	tra
large	grand	grande	groß	grande
medium	moyen	mediano	mittel	medio
small	petit	pequeño	klein	piccolo
tall	grand	alto	groß	alto
short	petit	bajo	kurz	basso
fat	gros	gordo	dick	grasso
thin	mince	delgado	dünn	magro
old	vieux	viejo	alt	vecchio
new	nouveau	nuevo	neu	nuovo
wide	large	ancho	breit	largo
narrow	étroit	estrecho	schmal	stretto
full	plein	lleno	voll	pieno
empty	vide	vacío	leer	vuoto
bad	mauvais	malo	böse	male
good	bon	bueno	gut	buono
fast	rapide	rápido	schnell	rapido

slow	lent	despacio	langsam	lento
happy	heureux	feliz	glücklich	felice
sad	triste	triste	traurig	infelice
dark	foncé	oscuro	dunkel	scuro
light	clair	claro	hell	chiaro
sharp	affilé	puntiagudo	scharf	tagliente
dull	émoussé	sin punta	stumpf	non tagliente
soft	doux	suave	weich	morbido
hard	dur	duro	hart	duro
heavy	lourd	pesado	schwer	pesante
light	léger	ligero	leicht	leggero
hot	chaud	caliente	heiß	caldo
cold	froid	frío	kalt	freddo
dirty	sale	sucio	schmutzig	sporco
clean	propre	limpio	sauber	pulito
left	gauche	izquierdo	link	sinistro
right	droite	derecho	recht	destro
wet	mouillé	mojado	naß	umido
dry	sec	seco	trocken	secco
easy	facile	fácil	einfach	facile
difficult	difficile	difícil	schwierig	difficile
open	ouvert	abierto	offen	aperto
closed	fermé	cerrado	zu	chiuso
long	long	largo	lang	lungo
short	court	corto	kurz	corto
on	allumé	encendido	an	acceso
off	éteint	apagado	aus	spento

27. Action Words

QUESTIONS ABOUT THE PICTURES

1. What actions do you do with food?
2. *(upper right)* What are the children doing with the ball?
3. *(upper left)* Why is the girl crying?
4. *(upper left)* Why is the girl laughing?
5. *(center)* What is the boy looking for?
6. *(lower left)* Describe what is happening in the sell and buy pictures.
7. *(lower right)* Describe what is happening in the break and fix pictures.
8. Which are actions that you do often?
9. Which are actions that you have never done?
10. What things don't you know how to do?

ACTION STORIES

Possible topics: getting ready in the morning, taking a walk in the park, what you do after school

Example: Getting ready in the morning

1. It's the alarm clock. Listen to the ring! 2. Get out of bed. 3. Wash your face. 4. Go to the bedroom. 5. Put on your clothes. 6. Look under the bed for your shoe. 7. Good! I've found it! 8. Put on the shoe. 9. Go to the kitchen. 10. Drink some juice. 11. Get some cereal. 12. Go out of the house and close the door.

GROUP ACTIVITIES

1. Classifying

Have students name as many actions from the pictures as they can for each of the following categories: things you do in school, things you can do in the park, verbs that are opposites, what you do before you come to school, what you do after you leave school, things you can do with a ball, things you do to keep clean, things you can do to food.

2. Pantomime

Have students pantomime doing the activities in the pictures. Have the rest of the group guess the action. Extend the activity by using the pantomimes to introduce the nouns that go with the verbs and the correct syntax for use of the verbs. Encourage the class to answer in complete sentences. Example: He's throwing a ball. He's opening a box. He's playing the trumpet.

3. What Do You Do When . . .?

Have students work in pairs to do an information-gap activity. Prepare two sheets, one with actions and the other with situations in which the actions might be performed. The information that you put on one sheet should be missing from the other. Here is a sample of the complete information to appear on the sheets:

What do you do when . . .?	Actions
. . . you are very sad	cry
. . . you are tired	sleep
. . . you play baseball	throw
. . . you play soccer	kick
. . . you lose something	look for it
. . . you are hungry	eat
. . . you take a bath	use soap
. . . you write a letter	use a pencil
. . . you paint	use a brush

Pass out a different sheet to each of the students in the pair. The students are to complete their sheets by getting the information on their partners' sheets. They can do this by asking each other questions. Prompt the students to ask questions like: When do you (laugh)? The answer would be: I laugh when I see something funny.

WRITING

Have students do these activities independently or as whole-class or group activities.

1. List actions you have done.
2. List actions you haven't done.
3. Design your own robot. Decide what things it can and cannot do. Can it read, talk, write, etc.? Write about your robot.
4. Write about things that you do on a school day. Write about things you do after school.

5. Write about things that you have done on an unusual day. Perhaps it was the day you lost and then found your pet.

FOCUS ON LANGUAGE

Often a noun can be formed from a verb by the addition of a suffix. With the students, prepare a list of nouns that can be formed from the verbs in the unit by the addition of a suffix. Have students try to extend the list with other verb-noun combinations.

VOCABULARY

Action Words	Actions	Palabras de acción	Tätigkeitswörter	Le attività
to drink	boire	beber	trinken	bere
to eat	manger	comer	essen	mangiare
to sleep	dormir	dormir	schlafen	dormire
to wash (oneself)	se laver	lavarse	waschen	lavarsi
to skate	faire du patin	patinar	eislaufen	pattinare
to come	venir	venir	kommen	venire
to go	aller	ir	gehen	andare
to throw	jeter	tirar	verfen	gettare
to catch	attraper	recoger	fangen	prendere
to watch	regarder	mirar	anschauen	guardare
to fall	tomber	caerse	fallen	cadere
to cry	pleurer	llorar	weinen	piangere
to laugh	rire	reírse	lachen	ridere
to fly	voler	volar	fliegen	volare
to write	écrire	escribir	schreiben	scrivere
to sing	chanter	cantar	singen	cantare
to talk	parler	hablar	reden	parlare
to kick	donner un coup de pied	patear	kicken	dare un calcio
to listen (to)	écouter	escuchar	zuhören	ascoltare
to think	penser	pensar	denken	pensare
to read	lire	leer	lesen	leggere
to play (a game)	jouer à	jugar	spielen	gioccare
to play (an instrument)	jouer de	tocar	spielen	suonare
to sit down	s'asseoir	sentarse	sich hinsetzen	sedersi
to stand up	se lever	ponerse de pie	aufstehen	alzarsi in piedi
to roar	rugir	rugir	brüllen	ruggire
to dig	creuser	cavar	graben	scavare
to pour	arroser	regar	gießen	innaffiare
to juggle	jongler	hacer juegos malabares	jonglieren	fare giochi
to point (at)	montrer du doigt	señalar	deuten (auf)	mostrare
to dance	danser	bailar	tanzen	ballare

to walk	marcher	caminar	zu Fuß gehen	camminare
to run	courir	correr	laufen	correre
to climb	grimper	subir	klettern	salire
to jump	sauter	saltar	springen	saltare
to look for	chercher	buscar	suchen	cercare
to find	trouver	encontrar	finden	trovare
to give	donner	dar	geben	dare
to receive	recevoir	recibir	bekommen	ricevere
to cut	couper	cortar	schneiden	tagliare
to drive	conduire	manejar	fahren	guidare
to push	pousser	empujar	stoßen	spingere
to sell	vendre	vender	verkaufen	vendere
to buy	acheter	comprar	kaufen	comprare
to ski	faire du ski	esquiar	schifahren	sciare
to cook	faire la cuisine	cocinar	kochen	cucinare
to open	ouvrir	abrir	öffnen	aprire
to close	fermer	cerrar	zumachen	chiudere
to take a bath	prendre un bain	bañarse	baden	bagnarsi
to teach	enseigner	enseñar	lehren	insegnare
to dive	plonger	saltar (al agua)	tauchen	tuffare
to swim	nager	nadar	schwimmen	nuotare
to paint	peindre	pintar	malen (a picture)	dipingere
to draw	dessiner	dibujar	zeichnen	disegnare
to ride a bicycle	faire du vélo	montar en bicicleta	Fahrrad fahren	andare a bicicletta
to break	casser	romper	brechen	rompere
to fix	réparer	arreglar	reparieren	aggiustare
to carry	porter	llevar	tragen	portare
to pull	tirer	tirar	ziehen	tirare
to wait	attendre	esperar	warten	aspettare

28. Colors

QUESTIONS ABOUT THE PICTURE

1. Name the colors you are wearing.
2. Name the colors of four things in the classroom.
3. Name the colors of the flag of the country you are studying.
4. What color is the sky?
5. What colors are coins?
6. *(Have students look at one or more of the scenes, preferably from units they have studied.)* What color is the . . .?
7. What color would you like your own room to be?
8. What's your favorite color?

ACTION STORIES

Have individual students touch pictures/objects with the colors you name.

GROUP ACTIVITIES

1. Classroom Colors

Have students name the colors of objects in the classroom. Encourage use of complete sentences.

Example: This notebook is red. This crayon is yellow.

2. Trivia Game

Name common objects. The students are to name the color of each object. You might want to divide the class/group into teams and give points for correct answers.

Possible objects: apple, banana, pear, lemon, grass, snow, clouds, vanilla ice cream, ketchup, colors of the flag (of target language), tree, zebra, polar bear, turtle, frog.

3. Chanting

With students, prepare sentences describing the colors of things in the classroom. Have students chant the sentences.

Example: Our desks, desks, desks are brown, brown, brown.

Then have students prepare sentences with the colors of things they have. They are to chant the sentences.

Example: My bike, bike, bike is red, red, red.

4. Color Hunt

Divide students into groups. Give students the names of several colors. They are to write the names of all the objects that they find with the color in some environment: the classroom, the cafeteria, or outside of school. Give the students a set time to complete the task. Once they have finished, determine which group has found the most objects.

WRITING

Have students do these activities independently or as whole-class or group activities.

1. Make a color book. On each page or set of pages, write the name of a color. Then draw objects that have that color and label them.
2. *(Other transparencies in the program or from magazines are used in this activity. This activity reinforces the position of adjectives before or after nouns.)* Write down the colors of objects in the picture. Write both the color and the noun.

FOCUS ON LANGUAGE

1. Present/review the position of adjectives before or after nouns and agreement in form with nouns (if any).
2. Each language has idioms that contain colors. Often lists of these can be found in idiom books. Present some of the idioms to the class. For example, in English, some idioms with colors are *to feel blue, out of the blue, white elephant, to have a green thumb, to put out the red carpet.*

VOCABULARY

Colors	Les couleurs	Los colores	Die Farben	Colori
white	blanc	blanco	weiß	bianco
gray	gris	gris	grau	grigio
black	noir	negro	schwarz	nero
red	rouge	rojo	rot	rosso
purple	violet	morado	lila	viola
yellow	jaune	amarillo	gelb	giallo
green	vert	verde	grün	verde
pink	rose	rosado	rosa	rosa
orange	orange	anaranjado	orange	arancione
brown	marron	café	braun	marrone
blue	bleu	azul	blau	blu
gold	doré	dorado	golden	dorato
silver	argenté	plateado	silbern	argenteo

29. Family Tree

QUESTIONS ABOUT THE PICTURE

1. Who is your father's mother?
2. Who is your mother's sister?
3. Who is your aunt's child?
4. Your mother is your grandmother's _____ .
5. If you are an only child, you have no _____ or _____ .
6. What is another name for grandmother?
7. How many brothers/sisters do you have?
8. Do you have many relatives?/Do you come from a large family?
9. Who is the oldest child in your family?
10. Are you older than your brothers and sisters?

ACTION STORIES

Have individual students touch the appropriate pictures as you give commands; for example, touch the picture of the grandpa, touch the picture of the father's mother.

GROUP ACTIVITIES

1. Classifying

Have students name as many relatives as they can for each of the following categories: relatives who are women or girls, relatives who are men or boys, relatives who are older than you, people who have children.

2. Chanting

With the students, prepare sentences that describe relatives.

Examples:

My uncle is my mother's brother. Or my uncle is my father's brother.

My sister is my mother's child. And my sister is my father's child.

Have students chant the sentences they have composed. For example, My sister, sister, sister is my father's, father's, father's child.

3. Who Is Who?

Find pictures in magazines or in storybooks that show groups of people who look as if they are related. Have the groups of students speculate on the relationships among the people. Groups can present and compare their answers.

4. The Family Album

Have students bring in pictures of their families and orally describe their relationships to the people in the pictures. If necessary, prompt students with language for the explanations; for example, *older/younger, oldest/youngest.*

WRITING

Have students do these activities independently or as whole-class or group activities.

1. Draw your own family tree like the one in the picture. Write the people's relation to you. Add their first names, too.
2. Describe the family of a character you have read about or seen on television. Tell about the relationships (how many children in the family, the names in the family, who the aunts/uncles/grandparents are if you know, etc.).

FOCUS ON LANGUAGE

Present/review the language for describing ages: for example, the equivalent of He/she's _____ years old; I am _____ years older/younger than my brother.

VOCABULARY

The Family Tree	L'arbre généalogique	El árbol genealógico	Der Stammbaum	L'albero di famiglia
grandmother, grandma	la grand-mère, grand-maman	la abuela, la abuelita	die Großmutter, Oma	la nonna
grandfather, grandpa	le grand-père, grand-papa	el abuelo, el abuelito	der Großvater, Opa	il nonno
father, dad	le père, papa	el padre, el papá	der Vater, Vati	il padre, il babbo
mother, mom	la mère, maman	la madre, la mamê	die Mutter, Mutti	la madre, la mamma
aunt	la tante	la tía	die Tante	la zia
uncle	l'oncle	el tío	der Onkel	lo zio
brother	le frère	el hermano	der Bruder	il fratello
son	le fils	el hijo	der Sohn	il figlio
sister	la sœur	la hermana	die Schwester	la sorella
daughter	la fille	la hija	die Tochter	la figlia
cousin (m.)	le cousin	el primo	der Cousin	il cugino
cousin (f.)	la cousine	la prima	die Kusine	la cugina

30. Shapes

QUESTIONS ABOUT THE PICTURE

1. How many sides does a square/triangle have?
2. Which shapes are round or have a round side?
3. Which shapes are not round?
4. Which shape looks like a globe?
5. Which shape looks like a can?
6. Which shape looks like a block?
7. Which shapes have only two dimensions?
8. Which shapes have three dimensions?

ACTION STORIES

Have students draw in the air or on paper as you give commands: for example, draw a triangle, draw a circle, etc.

GROUP ACTIVITIES

1. Classifying

Have students name as many shapes as they can for each of the following categories: round shapes, shapes with four sides, shapes with three sides, shapes with more than four sides, three-dimensional shapes.

2. Shapes Around You

Name some everyday objects and have students identify the shapes. For more advanced or older students, have them name as many objects as they can for each shape.

Examples:

circle: coin, dish, clock, wheel

rectangle: piece of paper, envelope, picture

triangle: sail

oval: running track

sphere: ball, moon, globe

cylinder: can, pen

cube: block, room, television set, box

cone: ice cream cone

3. Shape Hunt

Have groups or individual students find as many things as they can in the classroom or immediate environment that are of the shapes that they have learned about. Have them make and compare their lists.

4. Shape Drawing

Give students directions to draw shapes that form objects. You can use objects from the units students have studied.

Examples:

a. Draw an octagon. Draw a line from the bottom of the octagon. *(stop sign)*

b. Draw a circle. Draw a rectangle under the circle. Draw three lines to connect the circle and the rectangle. *(a hot-air balloon)*

c. Draw an oval. Draw three lines from the top of the oval. Draw three lines from the bottom of the oval. *(insect)*

d. Draw a triangle. Draw a rectangle under the triangle. The bottom side of the triangle is the top of the rectangle. Draw 3 circles in the rectangle, one on top of the other. Draw a line from the bottom of the rectangle. *(traffic light)*

WRITING

Have students do these activities independently or as whole-class or group activities.

1. Draw each of the shapes you have studied. Label them.
2. Make a drawing that has shapes in it. List the shapes you have used in your drawing.

FOCUS ON LANGUAGE

Review/present the language for measurement. Provide rulers with the measurements commonly used in the target language country: inches/feet, centimeters/meters. Have students practice measuring items. Then have students draw triangles, rectangles, and squares, and measure the length of the sides.

VOCABULARY

Shapes	Les formes	Las formas	Die Formen	Le forme
square	le carré	el cuadrado	das Viereck	il quadrato
triangle	le triangle	el triángulo	das Dreieck	il triangolo
circle	le cercle	el círculo	der Kreis	il circolo
rectangle	le rectangle	el rectángulo	das Rechteck	il rettangolo
oval	l'ovale	el óvalo	das Oval	l'ovale
cube	le cube	el cubo	der Wüfel	il cubo
octagon	l'octogone	el octágono	das Achteck	l'ottagono
sphere	la sphère	la esfera	die Kugel	il globo
cylinder	le cylindre	el cilindro	der Zylinder	il cilindro
cone	le cône	el cono	der Kegel	il cono

31. Numbers

QUESTIONS ABOUT THE PICTURES

1. Which bear comes after the first, second, etc. bear?
2. What number comes after 2/3/10/100?
3. What number comes between 4 and 6/7 and 9?
4. *(Write a number on the board.)* What's this number?
5. What's 1 plus 2,etc.?
6. How old are you?/How many brothers and sisters do you have?
7. How many days are there in the week?
8. What's your telephone number?
9. What's your address?
10. How many letters are in your first name/last name?

ACTION STORIES

Give students commands to do activities a certain number of times.

Example: 1. Jump one time. 2. Turn around two times. 3. Touch your toes three times. 4. Clap your hands four times. 5. Take three small steps forward.

In turn, have individual students give commands to the class/group.

GROUP ACTIVITIES

1. Line Up

Have groups of students form lines. Have them identify their place in line, using ordinal numbers: I'm the first in line, I'm the second in line, etc.

2. Number Bee

Have a number bee. Quickly say a series of two or three numbers. A student has to say the next number quickly to stay in the game. You might want to do this as a team game, awarding points for each correct answer and letting students stay in the game.

3. Numbers in Math

Prepare a series of math problems. Make sure that students know the words for the operations (e.g., plus for addition, minus for subtraction, times for multiplication, divide for division). Have students orally say the problems and give the answers. Again, this could be a team game in which points are awarded for correct answers.

4. Treasure Hunt

Prepare a list of things in the classroom or some limited immediate environment; for example, windows, desks, books on shelves, erasers, wastebaskets, etc. Present the list to individuals or groups of students. Students are to indicate the number of such things that they can locate. Determine which group has produced the most accurate list.

5. Trivia Game

Prepare a list of things that have a set number with which students will be familiar: number of days in a week, months in a year, days in January, weeks in a year, players on a baseball team, legs on an insect, wheels on a bicycle, grams in a kilogram, inches in a foot, pennies in a dollar (use target language currency), sides of a triangle/square/octagon, planets in the solar system, continents on the Earth, states in the United States. Present the list to groups of students to complete. Determine which group has produced the most accurate list.

6. Information-Gap Activity

Obtain the prices of at least ten to fifteen items in a country in which the target language is spoken. Prepare two columns of information for an information-gap activity, one column having the names of the objects and the other their prices. Prepare two sheets containing the information in the columns. Information that is on one sheet should be missing from the other. Pass out a different sheet to each student in a pair. Have students complete their sheets by getting the information on their partners' sheets. They can do this by asking questions and saying numbers and prices. They should ask questions like the following: *How much is the . . .?*

WRITING

Have students do these activities independently or as whole-class or group activities.

1. *(Prepare a sheet in which there are rows of objects, each row containing a different number of items.)* Write the number of things in each row.

2. Write a description of yourself in which you use as many numbers as you can. Here's a start:
   I am _____ years old. I have _____ brothers and _____ sisters. My telephone number is _____ and I live at _____ . Every morning I get up at _____ o'clock. It takes me _____ minutes to get ready for school. School begins at _____ . There are _____ students in my class. I have _____ good friends. I collect things. I have _____ marbles and _____ baseball cards.

FOCUS ON LANGUAGE

Review/present rules for the formation of the plural in the target language or present some irregular plurals.

VOCABULARY

Numbers	Les nombres	Las números	Die Nummern	I numeri
Ordinal Numbers	**Les nombres ordinaux**	**Los números ordinales**	**die Ordnungszahlen**	**I Numeri ordinali**
first	premier	primero	erst-	primo
second	deuxième	segundo	zweit-	secondo
third	troisième	tercero	dritt-	terzo
fourth	quatrième	cuarto	viert-	quarto
fifth	cinquième	quinto	fünft-	quinto
sixth	sixième	sexto	sechst-	sesto
seventh	septième	séptimo	siebt-	settimo
eighth	huitième	octavo	acht-	ottavo
ninth	neuvième	noveno	neunt-	nono
tenth	dixième	décimo	zehnt-	decimo
Cardinal Numbers	**Les nombres cardinaux**	**Los números cardinales**	**die Grundzahlen**	**I numeri cardinali**
zero	zéro	cero	null	lo zero
one-half	un demi	la mitad	ein halb	una metà
one	un	uno	eins	uno
two	deux	dos	zwei	due
three	trois	tres	drei	tre
four	quatre	cuatro	vier	quattro
five	cinq	cinco	fünf	cinque
six	six	seis	sechs	sei
seven	sept	siete	sieben	sette
eight	huit	ocho	acht	otto
nine	neuf	nueve	neun	nove
ten	dix	diez	zehn	dieci
eleven	onze	once	elf	undici
twelve	douze	doce	zwölf	dodici
thirteen	treize	trece	dreizehn	tredici
fourteen	quatorze	catorce	vierzehn	quattordici
fifteen	quinze	quince	fünfzehn	quindici
sixteen	seize	dieciséis	sechzehn	sedici

seventeen	dix-sept	diecisiete	siebzehn	diciassette
eighteen	dix-huit	dieciocho	achtzehn	diciotto
nineteen	dix-neuf	diecinueve	neunzehn	diciannove
twenty	vingt	veinte	zwanzig	venti
twenty-one	vingt et un	veintiuno	einundzwanzig	ventuno
twenty-two	vingt-deux	veintidós	zweiundzwanzig	ventidue
twenty-three	vingt-trois	veintitrés	dreiundzwanzig	ventitrè
twenty-four	vingt-quatre	veinticuatro	vierundzwanzig	ventiquattro
twenty-five	vingt-cinq	veinticinco	fünfundzwanzig	venticinque
twenty-six	vingt-six	veintiséis	sechsundzwanzig	ventisei
twenty-seven	vingt-sept	veintisiete	siebenundzwanzig	ventisette
twenty-eight	vingt-huit	veintiocho	achtundzwanzig	ventotto
twenty-nine	vingt-neuf	veintinueve	neunundzwanzig	ventinove
thirty	trente	treinta	dreißig	trenta
thirty-one	trente et un	treinta y uno	einunddreißig	trentuno
thirty-two	trente-deux	treinta y dos	zweiunddreißig	trentadue
thirty-three	trente-trois	treinta y tres	dreiunddreißig	trentatrè
thirty-four	trente-quatre	treinta y cuatro	vierunddreißig	trentaquattro
thirty-five	trente-cinq	treinta y cinco	fünfunddreißig	trentacinque
thirty-six	trente-six	treinta y seis	sechsunddreißig	trentasei
thirty-seven	trente-sept	treinta y siete	siebenunddreißig	trentasette
thirty-eight	trente-huit	treinta y ocho	achtunddreißig	trentotto
thirty-nine	trente-neuf	treinta y nueve	neununddreißig	trentanove
forty	quarante	cuarenta	vierzig	quaranta
forty-one	quarante et un	cuarenta y uno	einundvierzig	quarantuno
forty-two	quarante-deux	cuarenta y dos	zweiundvierzig	quarantadue
forty-three	quarante-trois	cuarenta y tres	dreiundvierzig	quarantatrè
forty-four	quarante-quatre	cuarenta y cuatro	vierundvierzig	quarantaquattro
forty-five	quarante-cinq	cuarenta y cinco	fünfundvierzig	quarantacinque
forty-six	quarante-six	cuarenta y seis	sechsundvierzig	quarantasei
forty-seven	quarante-sept	cuarenta y siete	siebenundvierzig	quarantasette
forty-eight	quarante-huit	cuarenta y ocho	achtundvierzig	quarantotto
forty-nine	quarante-neuf	cuarenta y nueve	neunundvierzig	quarantanove
fifty	cinquante	cincuenta	fünfzig	cinquanta

fifty-one	cinquante et un	cincuenta y uno	einundfünfzig	cinquantuno
fifty-two	cinquante-deux	cincuenta y dos	zweiundfünfzig	cinquantadue
fifty-three	cinquante-trois	cincuenta y tres	dreiundfünfzig	cinquantatrè
fifty-four	cinquante-quatre	cincuenta y cuatro	vierundfünfzig	cinquantaquattro
fifty-five	cinquante-cinq	cincuenta y cinco	fünfundfünfzig	cinquantacinque
fifty-six	cinquante-six	cincuenta y seis	sechsundfünfzig	cinquantasei
fifty-seven	cinquante-sept	cincuenta y siete	siebenundfünfzig	cinquantasette
fifty-eight	cinquante-huit	cincuenta y ocho	achtundfünfzig	cinquantotto
fifty-nine	cinquante-neuf	cincuenta y nueve	neunundfünfzig	cinquantanove
sixty	soixante	sesenta	sechzig	sessanta
sixty-one	soixante et un	sesenta y uno	einundsechzig	sessantuno
sixty-two	soixante-deux	sesenta y dos	zweiundsechzig	sessantadue
sixty-three	soixante-trois	sesenta y tres	dreiundsechzig	sessantatrè
sixty-four	soixante-quatre	sesenta y cuatro	vierundsechzig	sessantaquattro
sixty-five	soixante-cinq	sesenta y cinco	fünfundsechzig	sessantacinque
sixty-six	soixante-six	sesenta y seis	sechsundsechzig	sessantasei
sixty-seven	soixante-sept	sesenta y siete	siebenundsechzig	sessantasette
sixty-eight	soixante-huit	sesenta y ocho	achtundsechzig	sessantotto
sixty-nine	soixante-neuf	sesenta y nueve	neunundsechzig	sessantanove
seventy	soixante-dix	setenta	siebzig	settanta
seventy-one	soixante et onze	setenta y uno	einundsiebzig	settantuno
seventy-two	soixante-douze	setenta y dos	zweiundsiebzig	settantadue
seventy-three	soixante-treize	setenta y tres	dreiundsiebzig	settantatrè
seventy-four	soixante-quatorze	setenta y cuatro	vierundsiebzig	settantaquattro
seventy-five	soixante-quinze	setenta y cinco	fünfundsiebzig	settantacinque
seventy-six	soixante-seize	setenta y seis	sechsundsiebzig	settantasei
seventy-seven	soixante-dix-sept	setenta y siete	siebenundsiebzig	settantasette
seventy-eight	soixante-dix-huit	setenta y ocho	achtundsiebzig	settantotto
seventy-nine	soixante-dix-neuf	setenta y nueve	neunundsiebzig	settantanove
eighty	quatre-vingts	ochenta	achtzig	ottanta
eighty-one	quatre-vingt-un	ochenta y uno	einundachtzig	ottantuno
eighty-two	quatre-vingt-deux	ochenta y dos	zweiundachtzig	ottantadue
eighty-three	quatre-vingt-trois	ochenta y tres	dreiundachtzig	ottantatrè
eighty-four	quatre-vingt-quatre	ochenta y cuatro	vierundachtzig	ottantaquattro

eighty-five	quatre-vingt-cinq	ochenta y cinco	fünfundachtzig	ottantacinque
eighty-six	quatre-vingt-six	ochenta y seis	sechsundachtzig	ottantasei
eighty-seven	quatre-vingt-sept	ochenta y siete	siebenundachtzig	ottantasette
eighty-eight	quatre-vingt-huit	ochenta y ocho	achtundachtzig	ottantotto
eighty-nine	quatre-vingt-neuf	ochenta y nueve	neunundachtzig	ottantanove
ninety	quatre-vingt-dix	noventa	neunzig	novanta
ninety-one	quatre-vingt-onze	noventa y uno	einundneunzig	novantuno
ninety-two	quatre-vingt-douze	noventa y dos	zweiundneunzig	novantadue
ninety-three	quatre-vingt-treize	noventa y tres	dreiundneunzig	novantatrè
ninety-four	quatre-vingt-quatorze	noventa y cuatro	vierundneunzig	novantaquattro
ninety-five	quatre-vingt-quinze	noventa y cinco	fünfundneunzig	novantacinque
ninety-six	quatre-vingt-seize	noventa y seis	sechsundneunzig	novantasei
ninety-seven	quatre-vingt-dix-sept	noventa y siete	siebenundneunzig	novantasette
ninety-eight	quatre-vingt-dix-huit	noventa y ocho	achtundneunzig	novantotto
ninety-nine	quatre-vingt-dix-neuf	noventa y nueve	neunundneunzig	novantanove
one hundred	cent	cien	hundert	cento
one thousand	mille	mil	tausend	mille
ten thousand	dix mille	diez mil	zehntausend	dieci mila
one hundred thousand	cent mille	cien mil	hunderttausend	cento mila
one million	un million	un millón	eine Million	un milione
one billion	un milliard	mil millones	eine Milliarde	un miliardo

32. A Map of the World

QUESTIONS ABOUT THE PICTURE

1. What are the names of the continents?
2. What are the names of the oceans?
3. What is the name of the line across the middle of the Earth?
4. What are the four directions?
5. What do you see in the north of Asia?
6. What is the name of the northernmost point in the world?
7. What two continents are completely south of the equator?
8. What continents are on the equator?
9. Which continent is the largest?
10. On what continent do you live?

ACTION STORIES

Have individual students point to the places as you give commands; for example: First, I fly to Europe. Next, I fly to the North Pole. Then I fly to Asia. I land on the tundra.

GROUP ACTIVITIES

1. Classifying

Have students name as many things as they can for each of the following categories: continents, geographical features, oceans, things in hot places, things in cold places.

2. Chanting

Discuss the various geographical features in the lesson. With the students, prepare sentences that describe geographical features.

Examples:

An iceberg is a huge piece of ice in the ocean.

A desert is a large dry place; it gets little rain.

A jungle is a hot place; it gets a lot of rain.

A volcano is a mountain that gives out fires and fiery rocks.

An island is land that is completely surrounded by water.

Have students chant the sentences they have composed.

3. Information Game

Have students work in pairs to do an information-gap activity. Prepare two columns of information, one with places and the other with descriptions. Write the information on two sheets of paper. Information that you put on one sheet should be missing from the other. Here is a sample of the complete information to appear on the sheets:

Places	**Description**
Africa	hottest continent
Pacific	largest ocean
Asia	largest continent
Antarctica	coldest continent
Australia	oldest continent
Sahara	largest desert
Nile	longest river
Greenland	largest river
Asia	continent with the most people
Antarctica	continent with the most ice

Pass out a different sheet to each of the students in the pair. The students are to complete their sheets by getting the information on their partners' sheets. They can do this by asking questions of each other. Prompt the students to ask this question: What is the. . . . (*hottest continent*)? Once the activity is complete, help students locate places on the map.

4. Group Project

Have students do research and describe one of the environments named in the picture: jungle, desert, polar regions, tundra. Lower-level students could draw a picture of the environment, labeling animals and plants, and could orally tell about the climate. Higher-level students could do a written report.

WRITING

Have students do these activities independently or as whole-class or group activities.

1. Draw a direction compass, showing at least four directions.

2. Plan a trip around the world. What places will you visit? How will you travel from place to place?
3. Draw one of the continents. Label places on it.

FOCUS ON LANGUAGE

1. Present/review the structure for describing directions; for example, the equivalent of *Europe is west of Asia*.
2. Present/review the forms for names of countries/rivers/mountains, which may vary in gender in the target language.

VOCABULARY

A Map of the World	La carte du monde	Un mapamundi	Die Weltkarte	La carta geografica del mondo
Africa	l'Afrique	África	Afrika	l'Africa
Antarctica	l'Antarctique	la Antártida	Antarktis	l'Antartide
Asia	l'Asie	Asia	Asien	l'Asia
Australia	l'Australie	Austrialia	Australien	l'Australia
Europe	l'Europe	Europa	Europa	l'Europa
North America	l'Amérique du Nord	la América del Norte	Nordamerika	l'America del Nord
South America	l'Amérique du Sud	la América del Sur	Südamerika	l'America del Sud
North Pole	le Pôle Nord	el Polo Norte	der Nordpol	il polo Nord
South Pole	le Pôle Sud	el Polo Sur	der Südpol	il polo Sud
Arctic Ocean	l'océan Arctique	el Océano Glacial Ártico	das nördliche Eismeer	l'Oceano Artico
Atlantic Ocean	l'océan Atlantique	el Océano Atlántico	der Atlantik	l'Oceano Atlantico
Indian Ocean	l'océan Indien	el Océano Índico	der Indische Ozean	l'Oceano Indiano
Pacific Ocean	l'océan Pacifique	el Océano Pacífico	der Pazifik	l'Oceano Pacifico
bay	la baie	la bahía	die Bucht	la baia
cape	le cap	el cabo	da Kap	il capo
canal	le canal	el canal	der Kanal	il canale
channel	le bras de mer	el canal	die Meerenge	il canale
desert	le désert	el desierto	die Wüste	is deserto
equator	l'équateur	el ecuador	der Äquator	l'equatore
fault	la faille	la falla	die Verwerfung	la faglia
glacier	le galcier	el glaciar	der Gletscher	il ghiacciaio
gulf	le golfe	el golfo	der Golf	il golfo
iceberg	l'iceberg	el témpano	der Eisberg	l'iceberg
icecap	la calotte glaciaire	el manto de hielo	die Eisdecke	la calotta polare
island	l'île	la isla	die Insel	l'isola
jungle	la jungle	la selva	der Dschungel	la giungla
lake	le lac	el lago	der See	is lago
mountains	les montagnes	las montañas	die Berge	la montagna
oasis	l'oasis	el oasis	die Oase	l'oasi
peninsula	la péninsule	la península	die Halbinsel	la penisola

plain	la plaine	la llanura	da Flachlandder	la pianura
river	le Fleuve	le río	der Fluß	il fiume
sea	la mer	el mark	die See	il mare
tundra	la toundra	la tundra	die Tundra	la tundra
volcano	le volcan	el volcán	der Vulkan	il vulcano
waterfall	la cascade	la catarata	der Wasserfall	la cascata
compass	la boussole	la brújula	der Kompaß	il compasso
north	le nord	norte	der Norden	nord
south	le sud	sur	der Süden	sud
east	l'est	este	der Osten	est
west	l'ouest	oeste	der Westen	ovest
northwest	le nord-ouest	noroeste	der Nordwesten	nord-ovest
northeast	le nord-est	nordeste	der Nordosten	nord-est
southeast	le sud-est	sudeste	der Süosten	sud-est
southwest	le sud-ouest	sudoeste	der Südwesten	sud-ovest

Notes

LET'S LEARN LANGUAGE DEVELOPMENT MATERIALS

Transparencies
Let's Learn Language Development Transparencies, available in Spanish, French, and All-Language Editions

Bilingual Picture Dictionaries
Let's Learn Spanish Picture Dictionary
Let's Learn French Picture Dictionary
Let's Learn German Picture Dictionary
Let's Learn Italian Picture Dictionary
Let's Learn Japanese Picture Dictionary
Let's Learn Hebrew Picture Dictionary
Let's Learn Portuguese Picture Dictionary
Aprendamos inglés, diccionario ilustrado

Monolingual Picture Dictionaries
Let's Learn English Picture Dictionary
Aprendamos español, diccionario ilustrado

NTC

For further information or a current catalog, write:
National Textbook Company
a division of *NTC Publishing Group*
4255 West Touhy Avenue
Lincolnwood, Illinois 60646-1975 U.S.A.